Ready-to-Use

CONFLICT-RESOLUTION

ACTIVITIES

for Elementary Students

Ready-to-Use
CONFLICT-RESOLUTION
ACTIVITIES
for Elementary Students

BETH TEOLIS

**THE CENTER FOR APPLIED
RESEARCH IN EDUCATION**
Paramus, NJ 07652

Library of Congress Cataloging-in-Publication Data

Teolis, Beth.
    Ready-to-use conflict resolution activities for elementary
students : over 100 step-by-step lessons and illustrated activities
that give grades K–6 students practical tools to solve
conflicts with empathy and feel like winners! / Beth Teolis.
        p.   cm.
    Includes bibliographical references (p.   ).
    ISBN 0-87628-918-9 (spiral wire) — ISBN 0-13-044970-9 (paper)
    1. Conflict management—Study and teaching (Elementary)—
Handbooks, manuals, etc. 2. Self-esteem—Study and teaching
(Elementary)—Handbooks, manuals, etc. 3. Peer counseling of
students—Handbooks, manuals, etc. 4. Bullying—Prevention—
Handbooks, manuals, etc. 5. Education, Elementary—Activity
programs—Handbooks, manuals, etc. I. Title.
LB3011.5.T46 1998
371.5′8—dc21   97-52356
                                                    CIP

Printed in the United States of America

10 9 8 7 6 5 4   10 9 8 7 6 5 4 3 2 1

ISBN 0-87628-918-9 (spiral wire)   ISBN 0-13-044970-9 (paper)

Attention: Corporations and Schools

The Center for Applied Research in Education books are available at quantity discounts with bulk purchase for educational, business, or sales promotional use. For information, please write to: Prentice Hall Career Special Sales, 240 Frisch Court, Paramus, NJ 07652. Please supply: title of book, ISBN, quantity, how the book will be used, date needed.

**THE CENTER FOR APPLIED RESEARCH
IN EDUCATION**
Paramus, NJ 07652

www.phdirect.com/education

DEDICATION

I began this book with the line from the song, "Colors of the Wind," "How high does a sycamore grow? If you cut it down, you'll never know." This reminded me of what we, as educators, have the power to do to a child's spirit. We can build it up or cut it down. Many children never realize their potential because they have been cut down. Others, thanks to significant people in their lives—many of whom are educators who encourage a positive identity in them—soar and lead meaningful, fulfilling lives.

I would like to dedicate this book to the memory of a young boy, James Lonnee, who will never realize his potential. As I wrote this book, I liked to think if an educator who touched his young life would have read some of the concepts in this book and *encouraged* him, helped him realize what he *could* do (he loved art) instead of what he could not do, had cared enough to give him the love lacking in his life that he would still be with us today.

ABOUT THE AUTHOR

Beth Teolis, B.S., M.Ed., Indiana State University, taught elementary grades for over 12 years in Indiana and in Toronto, Ontario. She noted repeatedly the correlation between children's levels of self-esteem and their academic and social progress. She now devotes her professional career to building children's self-esteem and conflict-solving skills. A member of the National Speakers' Association, she is an active keynote speaker and workshop presenter at educational conferences internationally and also loves doing student workshops.

Ms. Teolis has also written *Skills for Life Resource Guide* (Metro Separate School Board of Toronto, 1993) and *Ready-to-Use Self-Esteem & Conflict-Solving Activities for Grades 4–8* (The Center for Applied Research in Education, 1996).

Ms. Teolis is available for seminars, workshops, and consultive work through Life Skills Associates, 149 Coldstream Avenue, Toronto, Ontario M5N 1X7; phone 416-484-8113; e-mail jwt@blakes.cd or fax 416-863-2653. More important, she would like to know how this book is helping you to help your children!

ABOUT THIS RESOURCE

"How high does a sycamore grow? If you cut it down, you'll never know."
—"Colors of the Wind" by VANESSA WILLIAMS

Each child who walks through your classroom doors has the potential of achieving boundless heights academically, emotionally, spiritually, and socially. Then why do some soar while others are cut down early in the process so that they never realize their early potential? As an elementary educator, you play a vital role in this potential growth or regression. That role places you as a potentially significant encourager in a child's life. Children may not remember many of the facts you taught, but they *will recall the image they saw of themselves through your eyes!* The way you treat them reflects your feelings about them, often without spoken words.

Enabling children to recognize at least one positive strength within themselves and providing the necessary life skills to succeed in their personal and professional lives are the true seeds of growth given to your students as they leave your classroom. For example, what can we, as educators, do about the lack of empathy and respect for themselves and others that we are seeing in our children? *We can do so much!*

We can begin by helping our children to feel secure and free from physical and emotional harm in our classrooms as we build feelings of trust and safety, the basis of Maslow's Hierarchy of Needs. Children are then ready to build positive identities, to recognize their strengths, and to accept their limitations. If this foundation of self-esteem is not learned outside of school or in previous classrooms, then *it's up to you to begin teaching it.* Otherwise, these children may never have an opportunity to know even one positive quality about themselves or to succeed in any, however small, way.

If insecure, low self-esteem children are expected to suddenly deal with their outer-directed anger before they have dealt with their inner-directed anger, all involved in conflict solving will become frustrated! These children are *lacking the foundation needed to learn conflict-solving skills.* The children who do *not* have feelings of security and positive identity too often turn out to be the statistics for school dropouts, suicide and drug and alcohol abuse. Or they may become members of gangs in order to gain a feeling of affiliation they are otherwise unable to find. Skills for dealing with outer-directed anger and conflicts with others are taught once this foundation has been formed.

HOW THIS RESOURCE IS ORGANIZED

Ready-to-Use Conflict-Resolution Activities for Elementary Students offers teachers and counsellors a unique activities program filled with practical tools, strategies and techniques to build children's conflict-resolution skills. You will find role-plays, anti-bullying activities, empathy activities, conflict-resolution celebration ideas, and more to meet the needs of your diverse student population.

Organized into four sections, the first section addresses *your* needs while the other three address student needs. Students will encounter the unusual activities of Wilbert, a colorful character who finds himself in unpredictable situations that many can identify with. Students need to help Wilbert so that he and everyone else has a win-win experience.

Numerous illustrated worksheets can be easily copied and used with students individually, in small groups, or as a whole class. Following is a brief summary of each section and its unique features.

Section 1:

In order to fulfill the task of teaching conflict-solving skills to your students, you need to model the behavior yourself. Intended as a refresher for your own self-esteem, anger management, and conflict-solving skills, this resource begins with a section dedicated to your own personal needs, *a time for you!* Some of the educator empowerment activities include:

- Replacing negative thoughts with positive self-talk
- Creating your own personal treasure chest of affirmations
- Having a "fast forward" in which a student writes a letter to you
- Staying on course with your goal setting
- Pushing aside aggressive behavior and handling conflicts assertively
- Learning how you can get out of your comfort zone to obtain what you want
- Realizing positive qualities your peers see in you
- Becoming aware of your anger patterns, triggers, and traps

Section 2:

In order to provide a foundation for students to deal with outer-directed anger, they first need to deal with their inner-directed anger. This section includes activities for the following skills:

- Enabling children to recognize positive things about themselves
- Teaching the skills of complimenting and receiving their compliments
- Developing responsibility for their own actions and accepting consequences
- Learning the qualities others like and how to develop those qualities
- Developing and upholding their values
- Understanding the emotional ups and downs of their feelings
- Learning the skills of communicating clearly, openly and assertively

Section 3:

After providing the groundwork for dealing with their inner-directed anger, conflict-solving activities are provided to deal with students' outer-directed anger toward others. Activities provide the following skills:

- Becoming aware of the five conflict styles
- Learning the patterns, stages, trigger,s and traps of anger
- Realizing how anger escalates and can hurt others
- Understanding the feelings of others in a conflict

- Learning the issues, communication, and feelings in a conflict
- Solving a problem with creative solutions
- Role-playing and discussing everyday conflicts to develop empathy for others
- Discussing undesirable ways of handling anger
- Learning the steps of peer mediation
- Learning the difference between aggression and assertion
- Knowing the roles of the bully, the victim, and the watcher in bullying
- Making anti-bullying a schoolwide goal
- Holding a celebration of conflict resolution activities

Section 4:

This section contains anti-bullying activities all the students in the school can use. "Bully Busters" activities make your students aware of what they can do to prevent bullying in your school. Information for your own ideas to deal with bullies is provided in "Teachers' Bully Busters." All the information you will need to get you started to set up a classroom or schoolwide Conflict Resolution Celebration is provided . Enrolling your students' parents as partners in teaching conflict-solving skills is made convenient with letters explaining to them what you are teaching their children. Invitations to classroom or school events are included. A home conflict-resolution menu is provided. Good News Network handouts and calenders along with ideas for monthly themes add a positive note to the school. Chill-Out charts are invaluable for making notes on your "time for two" chats with students. Class meeting set-up suggestions in a "menu" format are provided.

This section offers a special reading list compiled of resources for both educators and parents to read to first help them so they can then help their children with skills they can use to ultimately make conflict resolution more tender, more loving, and more caring for all involved.

Activity Sheets:

All activity sheets are preceded by teacher directions pages that contain the following:

- **Objectives** of the activity tell you at-a-glance the concept and the purpose of the activity.
- **Materials** you can easily get.
- **Step-by-step directions** tell you how to prepare, implement, and process the activity.
- **Bulletin board links** give you ideas for your classroom and halls.

How To Integrate These Activities Into Your Curriculum

- **Language Arts:** Creative essays, similes, and metaphors help students to express their feelings.
- **Drama:** Role-playing is one of the best ways to teach the skills involved in conflict solving. Scenarios that invoke empathy for "victims" is a crucial skill in conflict solving. Dramas depicting peer pressure, bullying, aggressiveness, and responsibility for their

own actions are provided. The put-down is role-played first, followed by the booster to build up the victim who has been put down.

- **Art:** Ideas for displays around the room, school hall collective art activities, bulletin board art captions, and student individual and cooperative art work are all integrated with the objectives of forming positive identities and solving conflicts peacefully.

- **Music:** Realizing that with children a song can paint a picture in their minds, suggestions for the use of music they can relate to are integrated with certain activities. A list of songs is provided for students to enjoy at a Conflict-Resolution Celebration or for graduations.

- **Creative Problem Solving:** Creative problems are given so that students can develop their lateral thinking skills. These creative-thinking skills will carry over to all subject areas as well as improve their abilities to solve problems creatively.

Do You Think You Can Make a Difference to a Child?

Do you find yourself saying, "I can only do so much!" about today's problems—bullying, lack of respect for self and others, threat of weapons, irresponsibility, lack of empathy for others, absence of values formation, insensitivity to violence, gang violence, conflicts resulting from racial and cultural stereotyping, gender inequity and lack of kindness towards others, to name a few. Use ideas in this and other resources, model the behavior you want your students to practice and show them the sincere interest you have in them. You will then be able to say, "I helped alleviate at least some of these problems with a few of my children. I *did* make a difference!"

Beth Teolis

ACKNOWLEDGMENTS

I want to start my acknowledgments at the very beginning, back to when my books were just a gleam in my heart. Without the publication of my first book, *Ready-to-Use Self-Esteem & Conflict-Solving Activities for Grades 4–8,* there would not be a second book completed here. It began with Rob Greenaway, then the President of the School Division of Prentice Hall Canada approaching Winfield Huppuch, President of the Education division of The Center for Applied Research in Education with the vision of resources for educators dealing with self-esteem and conflict resolution. Their vision was a step beyond publishing the basic core subjects as they realized students also need skills for life. I was then able to create what I have hoped are fun and meaningful activities to help children help themselves prepare for academic, personal and social success.

What an ideal support system I had under the leadership of Susan Kolwicz, my Education Editor, whose expertise guided me through the writing of this book. She made many of the suggestions for the activity pages. Nothing was ever a "problem" when I asked her. Diane Turso, Development Editor, patiently and expertly edited and put the rough manuscript together. I cannot give enough credit to the role these editors played in the development and production of this book. Publications Development Company in Crockett, Texas, then put it all together expertly with art and the print you see on the following pages.

Ideas for many of the activities and bulletin board and hall display ideas have come from my self-esteem and conflict-solving project schools in Toronto. I salute the following caring educators, those who gave extra energy, time and lots of heart: Marie Tait, Linda Dean, Pat Addison, Mary Stefanon, Charles Swindoll; the students of St. Paschal Baylon for their Conflict Resolution Celebration ideas under the direction of Mary Lou Sicoly, Performing Arts Itinerant for Metro Separate School Board; Ghada Sadaka, Claire Tassone, Franca Cancelli, Barb Ruhr, Nancy Pevcevecius, and the "good news" students of St. Simon's in Toronto.

My children, Cortleigh and Johnny, supported me as I wrote this book and my husband, John, did many of the computer graphics for this book. Alex Li and Carolyn Wilson assisted me with the illustrations for this book, hoping to appeal to the children. Johnny Teolis photographed me for the author photo. Cortleigh Teolis offered many activity suggestions and John Teolis scanned a majority of the art in this book, a huge job for which I am so grateful. We field-tested many of the conflict-solving concepts ourselves! (Yes, the TLC Recipe works but it's not always easy!!)

Most of all . . . I acknowledge *you,* the reader of this book, for going beyond the prescribed traditional core subject resources to realize that this, too, is a core resource that *goes to the heart of our teaching.*

CONTENTS

SECTION 3
Conflict-Resolution Activities for Your Classroom • 73

Problem Solving

Looking at a Problem from Another's Point of View

Empathy

Communicating the Best We Can

WANTED!!!! STORIES WITH HEART

I've been looking in the bookstores for a book written for educators about other educators with special stories they have to tell. I cannot locate one. So why don't we create one?

Educators are sometimes the only significant people to ever positively influence a child's life. In my books and workshops, I try to remind educators what a responsibility we have, especially for children to whom the *only encouragement they will ever receive will be from us!*

Do you have a heartwarming story you would enjoy reading yourself and would like to share with other educators? Would you like to read a collection of stories from other educators?

If so, we have a *perfect mix* because I would like to combine your stories with those I have collected over the past years at the many student and educator workshops I've enjoyed presenting. I realized so many children and educators have shared experiences others would enjoy reading.

Proceeds from the author's (Beth Teolis) royalties will go to help at-risk children in memory of the death of a young Ontario boy, James Lonnee. He was not fortunate enough to have been touched and possibly saved by a significant adult in his life. It is my feeling that a book such as this one, written by educators for educators may increase the awareness of just how significant they are in a child's life.

Authors of the selected stories for publication will receive a collection of all the selected *Teaching with Heart* stories. Please include your name, full address, phone number and tell how you work with children or the grade you teach. You will be contacted by Beth Teolis if your story is selected for the upcoming book written just for educators entitled, *Teaching with Heart Stories.*

Address:
Life Skills Associates International
149 Coldstream Avenue
Toronto, Ontario
M5N 1X7

Fax:
416-322-5270

Internet:
jwt@blakes.ca

Ready-to-Use
CONFLICT-RESOLUTION
ACTIVITIES
for Elementary Students

1
Conflict-Resolution Activities for Educators

"Conflict resolution begins with the self-awareness, self-caring, self-honesty, knowing what one wants and valuing it enough to speak up for it clearly. You are more likely to take responsibility for your actions and to accept criticism."

Sherod Miller, *Psychology Today*

IT'S MOVING DAY!

© 1998 by The Center for Applied Research in Education

Suppose you were told you'd won a prize—a brand-new wardrobe—that would be delivered to your doorstep in two days! After your initial excitement, what would be the first thing you would do? You would probably want to move out your old clothing and make room for the new wardrobe. This same method works to replace your negative thoughts with positive thoughts. Before you can make room for the new positive self-talk, you have to get rid of the old negative self-talk.

ACTIVITY:

To keep track of the negative things you say to yourself, when you get up in the morning have ready a large quantity of paper clips. Choose an outfit with two pockets or use two bags and mark one with a minus sign. Each time during the day you say something negative to yourself *about yourself,* put a paper clip into the other pocket or bag. Before bed, look into your negative pocket or bag holding the paper clips representing the negative self-talk and reflect how often you had those negative thoughts!

ACTIVITY:

You can also use the paper clip idea to keep track of the number of times you are negative with another person at home or a colleague or student at school. This activity will make you aware of how frequently you are negative with others. It is especially noteworthy to keep track of our negativity at home because often we are harshest with our loved ones. Then ask yourself if you need to have a "Moving Day" to get rid of your negative talk to others so you can replace it with words and gestures that make the people in your life feel encouraged, appreciated, and loved.

YAHOO! MY TREASURE CHEST

"For where your treasure is, there will your heart be also."

—Matthew 6:21

Do you give yourself "pats on the back" for things you do well? Or do you dwell on the mistakes you make?

Every night, in a special notebook, write five things you are proud of yourself for doing that day. Don't hesitate to attach symbols, or to create "yahoos" for things you are excited about! One could even be, "I did not feel guilty about relaxing this morning when I felt like I needed to." This will become a helpful time-management planner for you as you realize the things you feel most positive about are, or should be, your priorities. *Start off your writing tonight with five positive things you've done today written below in the "YAHOO!"* Cut it out and paste it in your notebook.

- -

MY ANGER TRIGGERS, TRAPS, 'N *TRAUMAS* LOG

Have you ever considered if there is a pattern to what *triggers* your anger and the *traps* you get "stuck in" when triggered? If so, is there a pattern you would like to change? For example, does someone in your life trigger angry feelings each time you have a conversation together or before you even speak? Are you trapped into reacting the same way each time you are triggered?

Issues and experiences we had as children that set us up for seeing and behaving in a certain way to a present conflict are *traumas*. A conflict is sometimes "haunted" by a trauma we have experienced in the past. For example, in a conflict you may not express the anger you feel but instead keep it inside (with clenched fists and tight lips) as a result of a habit of holding in your anger in your past. As a result of that passive, inner-kept anger, others may suffer by your behavior toward them or you may suffer from your repressed anger.

Complete the sentence stems below and learn more about your triggers 'n traps.

When I am angry usually I _____ and immediately I feel
_____ . Later I feel _____ .
_____ usually triggers my anger and I fall into the trap
of _____ . I see a pattern
of _____ .

Circle "can" or "cannot" below. If you cannot make changes in your triggers, write what you can do about your traps.

I **can   cannot** change my anger trigger(s).
I **can   cannot** change my trap(s) when I am triggered.

If I cannot change my trigger, here is how I will change my reaction to it, or the trap I often put myself into:

_____
_____
_____
_____

Write about a recent conflict when you were "haunted" by a past experience and reacted with behavior related to the past.

_____
_____
_____
_____

A LETTER TO YOU

Write a letter to yourself that a troubled student you taught would write to you 10 years from now. On the back of this sheet, write a letter you would write to a troubled student 10 years from now.

Dear _____ ,

_____

_____

_____

_____

_____

_____

_____

_____

_____

_____

_____

_____
(Signed)

PUSHING ASIDE AGGRESSIVE BEHAVIOR

"Speak when you are angry and you will make the best speech you will ever regret."

—AMBROSE BIERCE

Do you enjoy being with pushy or *aggressive* people? Not many of us do. How would you describe a pushy person? If you find it difficult to do, here is an easy way to describe a person who is pushy: Picture a line that is drawn, with the word "aggressive"on one side and "assertive" on the other side. In order to get what you want, if you hurt someone else, you have crossed over the line from the assertive side and into the pushy, aggressive side.

Getting what you want in a direct, firm manner in which nobody feels hurt is the *assertive* way to have your needs met. For example, if you need something from someone, make your needs known in direct, specific requests and assign precise accountability to others in those requests. Your goal will be accomplished and everyone's role in attaining it will be clearly defined.

Below write about some assertive and aggressive experiences you have had.

1. Write about an incident in your life and how you felt when you got what you wanted but you did so *aggressively* and someone was hurt.

   _____

   _____

   _____

   _____

2. Would you handle this incident differently now? _____ If you answer "yes," describe how.

   _____

   _____

   _____

   _____

3. Write about a time when someone you know got what he or she wanted but you were hurt. Rewrite the incident in a way that person could have gotten what he or she wanted in an *assertive* way.

   _____

   _____

   _____

   _____

DIAMONDS

"Precious jewels may be found within the wise, not around their necks."

—Greta Negel, *The Tao of Teaching*

Name _____

We are born into this world as shining diamonds. Sometimes our lustre fades and we need to be reminded what our sparkling qualities are. When others point out these qualities to us, we shine anew. Pass this diamond to five people who will write inside the diamond how they see you sparkle!

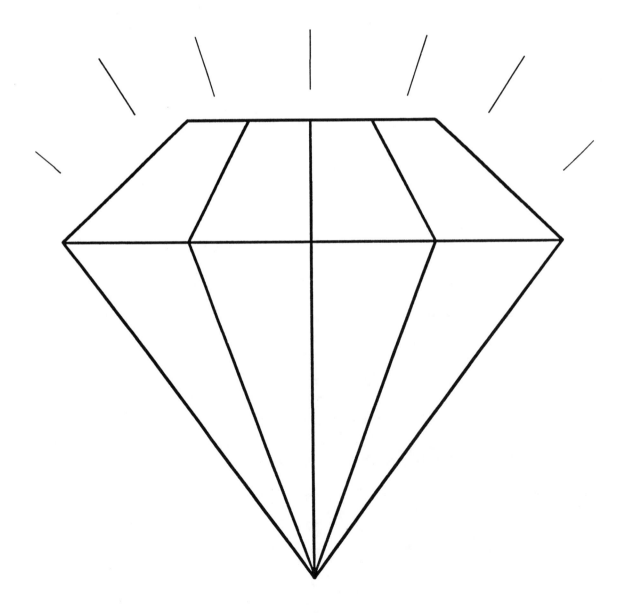

© 1998 by The Center for Applied Research in Education

Getting Out Of Your Comfort Zone

"You must do the thing you cannot do."

—ELEANOR ROOSEVELT

Does just looking at this title cause you some discomfort? Try this exercise: Fold your hands together and notice which of your thumbs is on top. Now shake out your hands and then fold them again, this time with the thumbs reversed. The thumb on the top before is now on the bottom. How does this new thumb position feel? *Responses:* "Uncomfortable." "Weird." "Like I want to go back to the first way I folded my hands."

What would happen if you continued to fold your hands in this new, uncomfortable way for the rest of the day, and then, the rest of the week? *Response:* "With some time, I would gradually get used to the new way of folding."

This is how it is with our *comfort zones* in life. We want to do things the way we are used to, that we feel comfortable with. It requires an effort to get used to doing things that at first cause us discomfort. So what do we do? We avoid getting out of areas in which we feel comfortable—our comfort zones—to take risks. Without taking *reasoned risks,* we close doors in our lives that could have opened up new challenges for us.

What have you done in the past year to get out of your comfort zone?

_____

_____

_____

_____

What have you wanted to do but have not wanted to take the risk?

_____

_____

_____

_____

What good idea you've had in the past are you now going to set as a goal to achieve?

_____

_____

_____

_____

ARE YOU HAUNTED?

There are three elements involved in conflict:

1. **Issues** (Problems that need resolving)
2. **Communication** (Present and past communication)
3. **Personal Feelings** (Ask, "What's *really* going on here?")

The *best way to handle conflict* is to wake up to the witness in ourselves as we watch our responses to those who irritate us.

Below write about the *responses you made* to the other person in a recent conflict:

_____

_____

_____

_____

_____

Below write about a conflict you have had where the real issue was not about what was going on in the *present*. It was really about something that happened in the past, *haunted by a past issue.*

What did the conflict *appear to be about*?

_____

_____

_____

_____

What was the issue *really about*?

_____

_____

_____

_____

Write how you will handle your "haunted" conflict the next time.

_____

_____

_____

_____

ARE YOU A *PUSHOVER*, PUSHY, or *JUST-ABOUT-RIGHT*
CONFLICT SOLVER?

You are in line for a book and a candy bar at the airport newsstand and someone (who you know is on *your* flight) steps in front of you with a newspaper and the exact change, while saying to the sales clerk, "I'm in a hurry to catch my flight. I have the correct change for my paper. Can you take it, please?" What would you do to handle the problem assertively?

_____

_____

_____

_____

You and your friend are at a restaurant when your vegetable soup arrives lukewarm. Would you eat the lukewarm soup or look for an assertive solution?

_____

_____

_____

_____

At a restaurant, a colleague asks you to loan her the money for her share of the dinner bill since her charge card is not accepted. You loan her the money. Now three weeks have gone by and no attempt has been made by her to repay the money to you! How would you handle this problem assertively?

_____

_____

_____

_____

Recall an incident you handled in an *aggressive* manner. You would now like to have handled it in an *assertive* manner. Write about how you would handle it if given the opportunity for a re-play.

_____

_____

_____

_____

WHAT THEY DIDN'T TEACH ME IN SCHOOL!

If you had been given problems to solve from unique, different angles during your school days, how creative would your problem solving be today? If you would like to improve your *creative* or *lateral thinking* skills, it's not too late! Start with the problems below and give them to your students, family, and friends. If your students receive a ten-minute creative problem-solving session every week, think about the ability they will have by the end of the school year! Why not make an overhead of the mind stretchers below and see how well your colleagues solve the problems.

Try a *different approach* to the mind stretchers below and watch your creativity emerge!

Mind Stretcher #1:

Circle and count how many "F's" appear in the paragraph below. _____
Clue: Just because you don't at first see the answer doesn't mean it isn't there! Look again from a different angle.

> **Finished files are the result of many finished years of scientific research combined with the experience of many years.**

Mind Stretcher #2:

A nursery school teacher has ten eager children all wanting an equal share of apples.
Problem: She only has nine apples! How is the teacher going to solve this problem?
Clue: Don't try to solve this problem in the old, mathematical way!

Mind Stretcher #3:

Find the pattern of the following numerals.
Clue: Don't try to solve this problem in the old, mathematical way!

8, 5, 4, 9, 1, 7, 6, 3, 2, 0

_____

Answers:

Mind Stretcher #1: There are 7 "F's." (Did you remember to circle the "F's" in the words "of"?)
Mind Stretcher #2: The teacher makes applesauce or apple cobbler.
Mind Stretcher #3: The pattern of the numerals is that they are in alphabetical order: Eight, Five, Four, Nine, One, Seven, Six, Three, Two, Zero.

© 1998 by The Center for Applied Research in Education

1–11. THE ROSE

Make a card with the rose page being the front cover and fold over to include the "secrets that shouldn't be kept" cut to place inside. The result—if copied on pale yellow or pink paper—is a meaningful handout for faculty meetings, conferences, PTA meetings, etc. Photocopy a card for each attendee.

Directions for Groups Using the Rose Card:

On the back of the rose card make a circle in the center of the page. Draw petals around the circle to create a flower. Think of a person you admire and put his or her name inside the circle. Then write the positive qualities you admire about that person inside the petals of the flower. Take about three minutes for this exercise. (Play "The Rose" by Bette Midler during this time.)

Now turn the card over to the rose cover and put *your own* positive qualities inside the rose. Allow yourself the same amount of time you used for the flower petals. When the time is up, count the number of positive things you wrote about the person you admire. Then count the number of positive things you said about yourself. Which person has more? If your admired person received more positive qualities than you gave yourself, ask yourself if you are in touch with all the positive qualities you possess. Try to decide what is holding you back from being your own most-admired person! Share this activity with special people in your life—family, colleagues, friends, someone you are most in conflict with, partners—and adapt the questions for use with *your students.*

THE ROSE

"It's the dream afraid of waking
that never takes a chance.
It's a heart afraid of breaking
that never learns to dance."
—BETTE MIDLER'S song, "The Rose"

SECRETS THAT SHOULDN'T BE KEPT *ABOUT ME!*

Write the "secrets" below privately or share them with a partner.

1. I feel my greatest strength is _____
2. I am most fulfilled _____
3. I have most fun _____
4. I appreciate _____
5. I miss _____
6. I would be found _____ on a day to myself.
7. I'd like to fling out and try _____
8. I feel sad when _____
9. I want to be remembered for _____
10. I hold most dearly _____

SECRETS THAT SHOULDN'T BE KEPT *ABOUT YOU!*

Share the "secrets" below with a student, friend, partner, spouse, or child.

1. My fondest memory of you is _____
2. Thank you for _____
3. I admire your _____
4. At times I need you to _____
5. I enjoy our _____
6. You are the most fun when _____
7. You do this so well _____
8. My dream for us _____
9. Your greatest strength _____
10. You are overcoming _____

2
Building the Groundwork for Conflict Resolution

"I love my job and I love kids. The most important thing I can do for students is to allow them a chance for self-discovery. I want them to understand and appreciate themselves regardless of the class material. Good teaching changes lives."

Mary Beth Blegen, 1996 National Teacher of the Year

2–1. PLAY MY POSITIVE TAPE AGAIN!

Objective:

Children learn first to be aware of their self-talk and, if it is negative at times, how to turn it into positive self-talk.

Materials Needed:

- "Play My Positive Tape Again!" activity sheet
- A class-favorite tape or CD
- Paper clips; pens; pencils

Directions:

1. Set the mood for this important lesson with a musical tape or CD your students enjoy. Choose a class favorite that always lowers the noise level when you play it! Seat your children in front of you if you have a carpet area. After a relaxed atmosphere is created, begin your discussion by telling children that they have imaginary tapes or their very own little headsets playing inside their heads all the time. Explain they may or may not be aware of them.

2. Tell them that these little tapes make good (positive) comments or bad (negative) comments to them. Introduce the "paper clip" method for getting in touch with these thoughts. To implement this, they choose an outfit with two pockets. All the clips are put into the right pocket. (Remind children a good way to remember left from right is if they are right-handed, that's the hand they write with. If they are left-handed, they use they pocket *they don't write with* to place the clips.) Their *left* pockets could be used to put one paper clip each time they catch themselves playing their negative tapes. At the end of the day, they should see how many clips are in their left pockets!

3. Explain to students the following points about self-talk: Another way of saying our little headsets play inside us is to call the talk *self-talk*. (Write this term as well as the words "positive" and "negative" on the board.) The comments are a result of what others have told them about themselves since they were very small. In order to know what the tapes say to them, they first have to be aware they are playing (using the paper clip or a similar exercise) so they can decide if they like and agree with the tapes or not. If the tapes are saying negative things about themselves, they may say they do not agree with them, after all, and would rather not play those negative tapes. Instead, they may say they would prefer to replace them with positive tapes.

4. Give children an example of a negative tape, such as "You're not athletic." Ask how they could change the negative statement into a positive one. *Response*: "You **can** play any sport if you work hard!" Ask students for other examples of self-talk they can change. *Response:* "Instead of my negative tape, 'You aren't any good in math!' I'll play this tape, 'I can improve my math if I study an extra 15 minutes each weekday and ask someone to help me.'"

5. Pass activity sheets to your students. Ask a volunteer to read the example at the top of the sheet, changing the negative tape into a positive self-talk tape. Tell students

that on the bottom of the activity sheet they can then choose two of their own negative tapes they will change to positive tapes. They are to first write the negative sentences they say to themselves and then rewrite them after changing them into positive sentences.

6. When activity sheets are completed, ask for volunteers to share their new positive tapes. Be sensitive to students who are reluctant to share their tapes. Some may have more negative self-talk than others and it may take repeated private talks between yourself and the child for the child to reverse the negativism.

PLAY MY POSITIVE TAPE AGAIN!

Do you like to listen to tapes? We play our very own tapes inside ourselves when we talk to ourselves. We call it *self-talk*. We need to say good *(positive)* things and stop saying bad *(negative)* things to ourselves. **Example:** Instead of saying to yourself, "I can't learn as fast as other kids," say "I *can* learn if I try hard." Below change two negative things you say to yourself into positive self-talk.

Negative Tape: _____

Change to Positive Tape: _____

_____

Negative Tape: _____

Change to Positive Tape: _____

_____

2-2. TICKLED PINK!

Objective:

Children learn to communicate positively about things that please them.

Materials Needed:

- "Tickled Pink!" actvity sheet
- Pink crayons or markers; pink glitter; *optional:* pink paper for copying

Directions:

1. Decide if you are going to ask your students to color their "feature presentation marquees" on their activity sheets pink or if you want to copy the activity sheet on pink paper. Or you may prefer to have them cut out their marquees from the sheets and mount them on pink background paper. **Note:** You may want to explain to your class that traditionally the color pink was considered a feminine color; however, in recent years it is more commonly used by both boys and girls.

2. After each child has received an activity sheet, explain what the saying "tickled pink" means. Explain that when we are very happy sometimes our cheeks get flushed or *pink.* Another way of saying we're pleased about something is to say we are *tickled.* "Tickled pink" is therefore a way of saying we are excited about something that pleases us. Explain that this activity will be a chance for them to write a "feature presentation" as if advertising for a movie or a play about what makes them happy!

   Note: This is also an activity in which the whole school could participate (if the topic "My School" is chosen) and have an entire *tickled pink* front hall!

3. Here are some ideas for use of the actvity sheet. Children complete the following topics to complete the sentence stem, "I'm tickled pink about.."
   - my classroom
   - my school
   - the way I handled this conflict
   - qualities about myself that make me happy
   - these special people in my life
   - doing this to help someone who felt hurt

TICKLED PINK!

When you feel happy sometimes, you can say you are "tickled" and your cheeks get pink. Another way of saying you are very happy about something is to say you are "tickled pink." In the marquee below write what you are "tickled pink" about in your classroom and your school for a *tickled pink* disply!

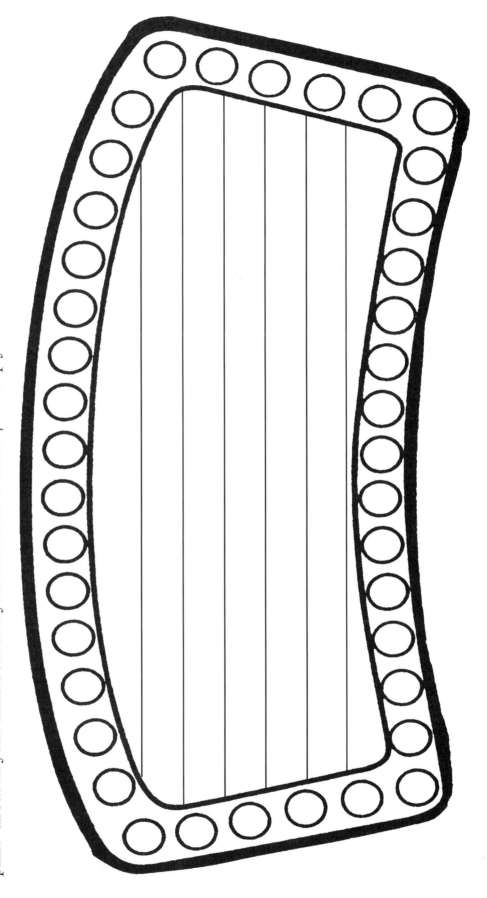

2–3. EXCLAMATIONS!
2–4. BALLOOSTERS
2–5. WOW

Objective:

Children are given the opportunity to give compliments to their peers in these activities. These will be pages many of your students will save and treasure.

Materials Needed:

- "EXCLAMATIONS!" "BALLOOSTERS" and "WOW" activity sheets
- Colored markers; pens; scissors; paste; *optional:* colorful paper for backgrounds if cut out, paste

Directions:

1. Discuss with your class qualities they like about other kids. *Responses:* "A good sport." "Keeps secrets." "Fun." "Helpful." As they volunteer answers, write their qualities on the board.

2. Tell students the activity sheets they are going to receive will give them the opportunity to tell others things they like about kids. Write the term "validation" on the board, explaining it is another word for a compliment. You may want to do each of these activities three different times (a different sheet each time with the same procedure) throughout the school year. The students are placed in different groups of six for each different sheet used so the opportunity is given for different validations. This rotation of groups takes some planning if you use all three sheets throughout the year.

3. Below are ideas for using each of the three activity sheets.

    "EXCLAMATIONS!" activity sheet: Ask students why they think these activity sheets have exclamation marks on them. *Response:* "An exclamation point shows excitement! We're going to write compliments about our classmates. I'm going to be excited when I read what they wrote about me!"

    "BALLOOSTERS" activity sheet: This activity sheet has balloons for children to write to the others in their groups their positive qualities. Explain the title is called "BALLOOSTERS!" as a fun way to express boosters on balloons. Ask students if they like the opportunity to tell their classmates compliments. *Response:* "We can tell our classmates something positive about them. When they get their sheets back, they will have good things written about themselves inside their balloons. And I'll be happy when I get my balloons back with positive things about me, also!"

    "WOW" activity sheet: Ask your students to pass the "WOW" sheet to the kids in their group to write how the child whose name is on the sheet "wows" them. These sheets are especially enjoyed by students as they create designs inside the WOW after it has been signed. They are then cut out and mounted on colorful paper.

    Note: The "WOW" activity sheets serve another popular validation activity. For Mother's Day students turn the page upside down to form the word "MOM." They write inside the letters all the positive qualities about their mothers that *wow* them—perfect for a Mother's Day gift!

4. The introductions for the three activity sheets are the same. For each of these peer-validation activities, decide how you want the groups in your class divided into groups of six. After passing out the activity sheets, the first step is to have each student write his or her name. If a name is not on a sheet that is passed, validations cannot be signed because students won't know whose paper is passed to them.

5. Give your children time to think and discuss how they would feel if they got their papers back and someone in their group had not signed anything about them. They would have received only three or four compliments instead of five. Ask for these feelings to be shared. *Response:* "I'd wonder why they passed on me. I'd be sad they couldn't think of even one good thing to say about me."

6. It is also important to make sure nobody writes a put-down on a child's sheet, thinking it would be funny. Ask how they would feel if they received their sheets back, excited to read what the kids in the group wrote and instead a put-down was on the sheet. *Responses:* "I might not let the other kids see it but I'd feel bad." "I would wonder which one said the mean thing about me. I probably wouldn't forget about it very easily." "I'd feel like they think I'm a loser." This activity requires your constant attention. You will need to watch all groups carefully to make sure the activity does not end up as a bad memory for any child who is ignored or put down by a classmate!

7. It's a good idea to play background music for this activity. With music, students don't feel the need to fill the silence while they are passing and signing. It also creates a calm mood if you choose a relaxing piece.

8. Make sure all groups are finished writing before you ask that all pages are passed back to their original owners. Notice the expressions on students' faces as they read what their peers have said about them! For an added glow, collect the sheets and add your own positive observations about the children that they will treasure.

   Note: Alternatively, these activity sheets could be used by individual students to write their positive qualities about themselves inside the illustrations.

Bulletin Board Link:

Here are some ideas for each of the three peer-validations activity sheets.

EXCLAMATIONS: A HUGE exclamation point is displayed in the classroom. Students' photos or pictures of themselves are drawn to go inside the point. Each student writes one favorite positive quality about himself or herself beside or under the pictures. Captions are "We're So Excited!" or "Here's the Point!"

"BALLOOSTERS: Display a colorful balloon for each student along with the compliments he or she received in their small group validation activity. Hang curled ribbon under each balloon. The caption is "We Give Each Other BALLOOSTERS!"

WOW: Activity sheets are displayed with the caption "Here's How We WOW Each Other." WOWs make an impact in the room when designs are colored inside the sheets, cut out, and mounted on colorful paper.

Name _____

EXCLAMATIONS!

Get into groups of six. Put your name on your page and pass it to the right to the other five in your group so they each can write inside your exclamation the *points they like about you!* You will do the same thing on each of their pages. See how you feel when you read the exclamations they have written about you!

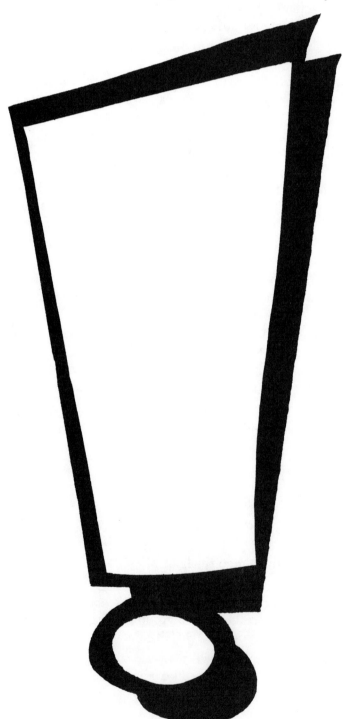

Name _____

BALLOOSTERS

Form a group of six. Pass your balloon sheet to each person in your group so that they can sign a booster about you. You can call these *balloosters!* Then write a *ballooster* for each one in your group.

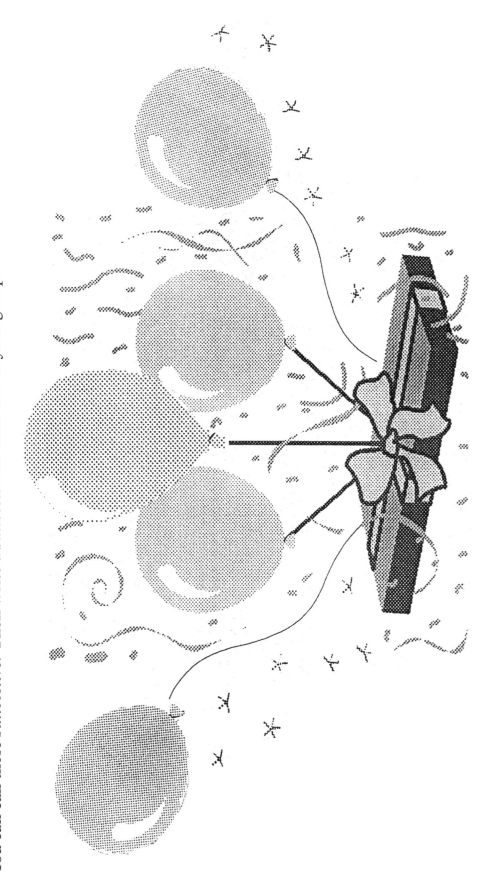

Name —————————

Date —————————

Form a team of 5–6 students. Put your name on your sheet, then pass it to your left for each person to write inside your "WOW" one positive quality that "WOWS" them! Examples: you are kind, lots of fun, try hard at sports, help at home. Decorate your WOWS and brighten up your classroom!

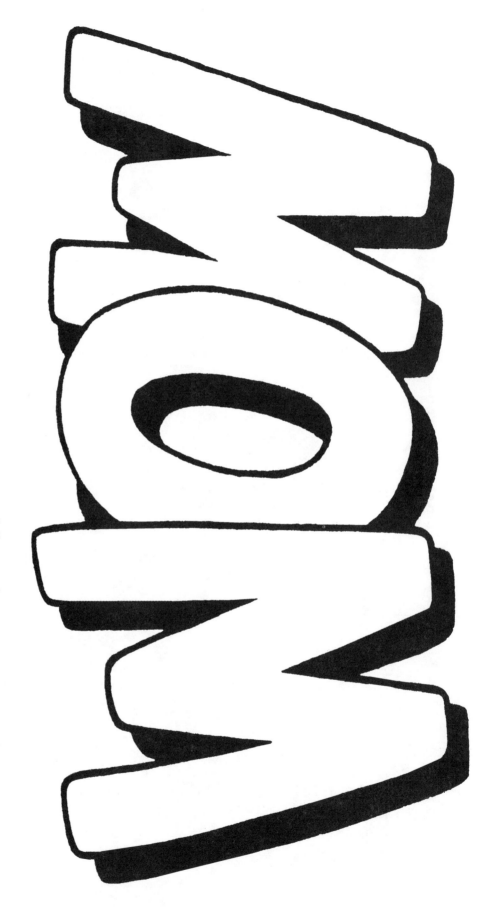

<h1 style="text-align:center">2–6. PRECIOUS PETALS
2–7. WHAT MAKES ME POP!
2–8. TUNE IN TO OUR TOP HITS!
2–9. I'M A HIT RECORD!</h1>

Objective:

Children compare the ease with which they make positive comments about others they feel are special and their ability to just as easily make positive comments about themselves.

Materials Needed:

- "Precious Petals" "What Makes Me Pop!" "Tune in to Our Top Hits!" and "I'm A Hit Record!" activity sheets
- Satin-sheen twisted ribbon in green, yellow, pink and white; blow dryer; colored cellophane; covered wires; moss and small clay pots; green construction paper; stapler; *optional:* yellow, white posterboard

Directions for "Precious Petals":

1. Pass out activity sheets. Ask a volunteer to talk about someone special and to tell the things that make that person special. Ask for these descriptions in one word. Write those special qualities on the board. Ask your class if they also like people with these qualities. (Responses will show the whole class that people with characteristics that attract others are fairly universal.) Then ask for several more things they like about others as you write their descriptions on the board.

   If a student gives a quality that is questionable, discuss it together. For example, a child may say that "bullying" is a "cool" quality, that other kids look up to a bully. Ask the rest of your class how many feel that the child who bullies others is someone who is "cool," someone they look up to and want to be around. (Responses will be negative.) Their responses will show the child that bullying is not a trait others like.

2. Explain to children they are going to write inside the petals of the first flower all the things they like about someone they admire. The person they choose may be someone they have never met, yet he or she has admirable qualities they have read or heard about, such as a sports figure who does a lot to help others as well as winning at sports. The person may also be someone they remember who has moved away who possessed positive qualities they still remember.

3. After you have given children time to write inside their first flower petals, tell them they are now going to do the same thing in the *next* flower petals. Explain that the difference is that they will be writing about positive qualities they feel *they* have! They will be writing about themselves. Try to give them about the same amount of time that they had for the first petals.

4. After the time is up, ask children how many found it easier for them to name positive things about someone else, or if it was just as easy, or easier, to name those good things about themselves. A show of hands will probably indicate that children found

it easier to name good things about someone else. This could lead to a discussion about the importance of being in touch with our own good qualities as well as people we admire.

Some may have learned that to acknowledge their special qualities is to *brag* about themselves. Distinguish in a class discussion the difference between children bragging and children feeling sure of their positive qualities.

5. Students cut out their flowers for their special people and paste them onto posterboard. Flowers are colored (or they may cut out with the sturdy background paper) and then wrapped in colorful cellophane (stapled onto the flower.) Green leaves and bows are then made to staple to the base of the flower. Flowers can be presented to their special people. They can do the same activity with *their own flowers* and hung together for a bulletin board display entitled "Our Class Has Petal Power" or "Our Precious Petals."

Art Link for "Precious Petals":

A more ambitious art activity is to make tulips with cut petal shapes from satin-sheen twisted ribbon (purchased at craft stores) and together with students use a hair blow dryer to open up the petals. The petal edges will turn toward the heat and curl slightly. (Painting the edges of the petals adds a nice touch.) Paste petals to covered wire and add green leaves. Place tulips in small containers covered with moss. These flowers can be placed outdoors. The satin-sheen twisted ribbon is waterproof. Alternatively, the tulips could be used instead of the above art idea for a display with the students' written or dictated words about their special qualities below each flower or written on the small plant containers.

Directions for "What Makes Me Pop!" "Tune in to Our Top Hits!" and "I'm A Hit Record!":

1. Follow the same directions for all of these activity sheets. Children write what they feel is special about themselves. You may want to choose one of the above activity sheets for the beginning of the school year, one for mid year and use the others later on to evaluate how some of the students who found it difficult to name any positive qualities about themselves have become aware of at least one or two positive qualities. Be sure to monitor these activity sheets by walking around the classroom to see if any students are unable to name any positive strengths they have. Spend some private time together discussing their special qualities you have observed.

2. Primary students enjoy making a large popcorn box (front of the box is all that is really needed) out of white paper and adding red or white lines to the box. Make large kernels for each child to write one positive quality written about themselves on the kernel. You may want to use these boxes and kernels for a short exercise break as children play "Pop-up!" Divide children into small groups. Each group takes turns crouching down behind the box. As one student holds the box and calls "Pop Up Now!," students pop up with their kernels displayed for the rest of the class.

Bulletin Board Links for "What Makes Me Pop!":

Popular classroom displays are made from "What Makes Me Pop!" activity sheets. Here are some wonderful ideas that have been used in many classrooms:

- Large popcorn kernels are cut out of yellow paper. Inside the kernels, students write stories about themselves with their own titles to complete the sentence stem, "A time I really sizzled was . . ." All the kernels are displayed on the bulletin board with the caption "Our Sizzlers!"

- Students color, mount, and cut out the popcorn boxes from their activity sheets for a colorful room display with the caption "What Makes Us Pop!"

- Cooperative groups of six pass their popcorn kernels to each other to write one positive quality about each child in the group. Have popcorn boxes and kernels made ahead of the activity, one box for each group and one kernel per child. Use white posterboard for the boxes and cut slits near the tops to place all the group's kernels, one for each member of the group, when they finish passing around their groups. The kernels are made large enough for five one-word compliments and a space for the child's name. Yellow posterboard makes colorful popcorn kernels. Each group member place his or her kernels inside the slits for the group. Display these in the classroom with the caption "Our Sizzling Qualities."

- Add popcorn kernels to the activity sheets for each child in your class. (You don't have to be artistic to do this!) Paste student class photos (don't forget your own) inside the kernels of the popcorn box. Copy one for each class member for a class keepsake. Display one in the classroom with the caption "Our Classroom Sizzlers."

Bulletin Board Link for "Tune in to Our Top Hits!" and "I'm a Hit Record!":

Children cut out ovals from their activity sheets "Tune in to Our Top Hits!" with their pictures drawn or photos inside and one positive quality about what they feel makes them a hit. Mount them on colorful background paper, if desired. Children enjoy coloring their records from "I'm a Hit Record!" activity sheets after writing or drawing a picture about what makes them a hit. Hang all the records together with musical notes or around a colorful jukebox for a fun bulletin board display. The caption for both activities is "Our _____ Class Hits!" (Fill in the number of students in your class.)

Name _____

PRECIOUS PETALS

Write a word in each of the flower petals of the first flower below to tell the things you like about a special person to you; for example: fun, loyal, kind. Then in the next flower petals, write the things you like about *yourself!*

Directions: Put an X in front of your answers below:

1. Did you find it easier to write things you liked about someone special than it was to find good things about yourself? _____ YES _____ NO

2. Did you write as many things you like about yourself as you like about someone special? _____ YES _____ NO

3. If you thought of more good things about the other person, ask others you care about to tell you special things about yourself that you may have missed. Then go back and write (or ask them to write) those special things in the petals of your **ME** flower.

Name _____

WHAT MAKES ME PP!

In the kernels, write the qualities that you feel have made you **SIZZLE!** *Examples:* good sport, fun, smart, witty.

 If we do not develop our good qualities, they will remain as unpopped kernels of corn!

Draw or paste your picture in the frame.

Tell why you're a **top hit** on your class chart.

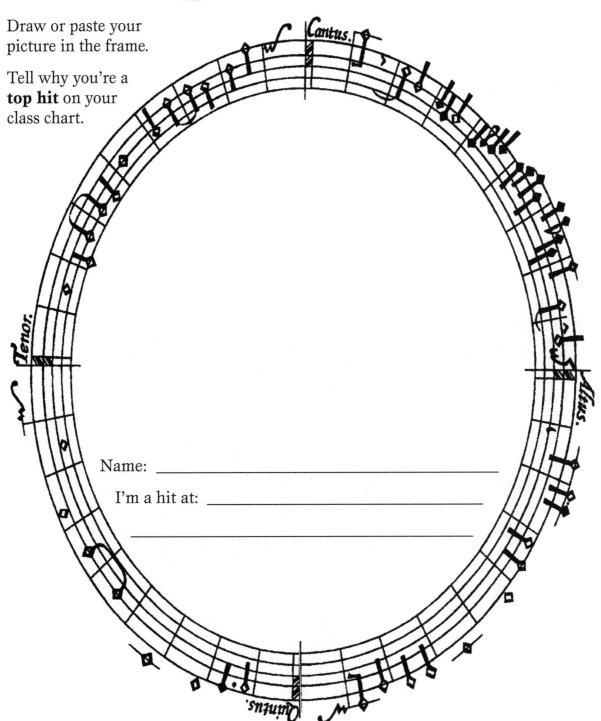

Name: _____

I'm a hit at: _____

_____

I'M A HIT RECORD!

Write a quality you have that makes you a hit. Draw or paste your hit picture in the record.

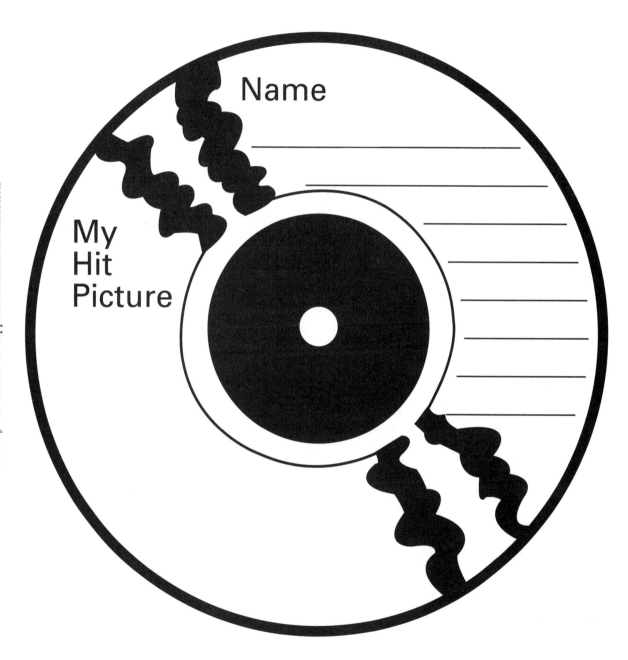

2-10. SNOWFLAKES

Objective:

Children learn that they each have unique qualities all their own. When they combine others' special qualities with their own, they learn they can accomplish a lot to help others.

Materials Needed:

- "Snowflakes" activity sheet
- Pastel markers, assorted colors of pastel paper for snowflakes
- *Optional:* white doilies, pieces of lace

Directions:

1. If you have a book about snowflakes, show your children pictures to enjoy. Discuss the pretty designs in the snowflakes. Tell them an interesting thing about snowflakes: there are no two snowflakes exactly alike, just as there is nobody else in the world just like them. Write the term "unique" on the board as you explain each child is unique with one-of-a-kind qualities.

2. Pass activity sheets to your class. If you copy the sheet onto a variety of pastel colors, you will have an assortment of colors to display. Ask children to write inside their snowflakes the things about themselves that make them special.

3. Discuss the quotation at the top of the activity sheet:

> *"Snowflakes are one of nature's most fragile things, but just look what they can do when they stick together."*—VERNA M. KELLY

This quotation is found in *It Takes a Village* by Hillary Rodham Clinton. Decide together a kind act you will do for the school or, if you have older students, for the community. For example, you may want to start a collection of items for needy children or have a class project to raise money for a special cause. If you do a snowflake display, include your class's kind act and a short description about it (written inside a separate snowflake.) Include in the display the quotation by Verna M. Kelly.

Bulletin Board or Hall Display Link:

Snowflakes make a lovely display with lace or doilies as background. Verna M. Kelly's quotation may be computer printed and hung at the top of the display with the caption, "Each One of Us Is Unique" or "Look What We Can Do If We Stick Together" or simply "Snowflakes." Include the quotation with your display.

SNOWFLAKES

"Snowflakes are one of nature's most fragile things, but just look what they can do when they stick together."

—Verna M. Kelly

Name _____

2-11. WALL OF LOVE
2-12. WE ARE FAMILY!
2-13. A LOVING VISUALIZATION

Objective:

Children will feel a sense of belonging within your school if you model and teach loving. It will help to create a sense of security for those cildren who may not receive loving outside of your school.

Materials Needed:

- "Wall of Love" and "We Are Family!" activity sheets; "A Loving Visualization" teacher-guided sheet
- Music for visualization (suggested: "Canon in D" by Pachelbel)
- *Optional:* butcher or other paper for "Loving Link" below

Directions:

1. A "wall of love" will be created using the activity sheet grams. (Or make "bricks" with students rubbing red crayons on paper over a real brick.) Decide if this will be a school-wide or your own individual classroom activity. You can create your own "wall of love" in your classroom or in the hall outside your classroom. Many schools have filled their front halls with grams from each student *and* educator in your school (parents, care-takers, and secretaries could be included also). An impressive display is to form the name or initials of your school with the cut-out grams or to form the words "peace" or "love." As visitors enter your school, they will see the loving front hall display!

2. Pass out a "Wall of Love" activity sheet to each student. For your "wall of love," students are to write why they feel their school is a special place for them. Alternatively, students write kind acts they can do for others to make the school a better place. Or they write why loving one another creates a peaceful school.

3. A popular use of the grams is to create a "wall of love" to honor the educators in the school, designated as an "Educators' Wall of Love." For example, the grams begin "Educators at _____ are special because they _____." Other than a "wall of love," the grams could serve any purpose you like such as, "We solve our conflicts at _____ peacefully. Here's how we do it. . . . " Students write what they are doing to resolve conflicts in your school.

4. Pass "We Are Family!" activity sheets to students if you want to include these in your "wall of love" along with the grams. Or you may decide to do this activity at a later time and not relate it to your "wall of love." Students are asked to choose special people for their musical notes. Those chosen as the special people in their lives are those people who *make the child feel special*. This recognition of others significant to them gives children a feeling of belonging.

   Note: For children who have a difficult time drawing and do not have pictures of the people they choose for their musical notes, give them the option of writing the names of the special people inside the notes.

A Loving Link:

Children make "radiant loving bodies" by tracing one another's outlines on butcher paper. Have the following questions on the board for them to refer to while locating the answers to the questions on their bodies' outlines:

1. Where would love live? *Responses:* heart, mind
2. Where would calmness live? *Responses:* mind, stomach
3. Where would power live? *Responses:* arms, legs, mind
4. Where would forgiveness live? *Responses:* heart, mind
5. Where would a loving touch live? *Responses:* hands, fingers

Alternatively, small bodies could be made by children and the same ideas above implemented.

WALL OF LOVE

Make your own wall of love by writing inside the gram below why you feel your school is a special place for you. Put all the grams in your class in the front hall and form the word "love" or the name or initials of your school. Create a wall of love for everyone to see!

My school is a special place because . . .

_____

_____

_____

_____

_____

WE ARE FAMILY!

Do you have some special people in your life? Draw or paste their pictures in the same numbered musical note.

1. This is someone special at home.
2. This is someone special at home or a relative.
3. This is a good friend.
4. This is someone (not in my family) who helps me and likes me.

1.

2.

3.

4.

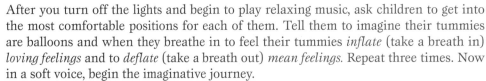

A LOVING VISUALIZATION

After you turn off the lights and begin to play relaxing music, ask children to get into the most comfortable positions for each of them. Tell them to imagine their tummies are balloons and when they breathe in to feel their tummies *inflate* (take a breath in) *loving feelings* and to *deflate* (take a breath out) *mean feelings.* Repeat three times. Now in a soft voice, begin the imaginative journey.

"You are taking a trip to the Land of Loving, a place where there is only love among people. This land is located wherever you want it to be. Imagine where it is. *(Pause.)* How will you get there? Star beams? Floating clouds? Superbus, train, or jet? Spacecraft? Underground tunnel runner? What other fun way would you like to travel? *(Pause.)* When you look around after you land, you see the special thing about the people is the way they treat one another. They treat others the way *they* like to be treated themselves! They listen the way *they* like to be listened to! They have differences, of course, because whenever people are together, they will always have differences. If their differences do turn into conflicts, these people handle them peacefully.

Look into your own heart now and think only loving thoughts about others as you breathe in love *(pause)* and breathe out mean thoughts. *(Pause.)* When we hurt or are hurt by others, our hearts may feel like they are shrinking. Is that how your heart sometimes feels? *(Pause.)* Does your heart feel like it's getting larger now as it fills up with love? *(Pause.)* People in this land tell you they learned how to be loving with others. They discovered that before they became the Land of Loving, they often took their anger out on other people, especially the people close to them. One day they learned how to control their angry feelings so they wouldn't hurt others.

The people in this land want to give you a gift to take home for you and others to be more loving. As you accept the gift box, you can't believe how little it weighs! It's as light as a feather. You were expecting something heavy, with maybe a big gold heart inside! After realizing the beautiful box is empty, you figure out the gift is something you need to be more loving, something you will put inside yourself. (*For older children say:* It is a quality you will need.) What is it? *(Allow silent time for children to choose their own gifts.)* Think how you will use it after you go home. (Pause.) You hug the loving people good-bye and you prepare to go home. You can hardly wait to share your gift!"

After the Visualization:

If children's eyes have been closed or if they have had their heads resting on their desks, ask them to open their eyes and to sit up slowly and stretch gently. Wait a few minutes before turning on all the lights while the music continues. When you feel children are ready, you can discuss the "gifts" they imagined receiving. Write the qualities or "gifts" on the board. Depending upon the ages of your students, responses may include: kindness, patience, empathy, helpfulness, loyalty, and thoughtfulness. Connect the qualities they received to how people who had these qualities could create a more loving world. Encourage them to draw what they imagined: the Land of Loving, how they got there, the people, the harmony they imagined. Ask your students how more loving would change your classroom . . . home . . . city or town . . . state . . . country . . . Follow up by asking them to do two loving things that day—one for someone at school and one for someone at home—and to share their loving acts the next school day.

2-14. CALL ME WHEN YOU NEED A FRIEND

Objective:

Children practice problem solving while learning that a good way to have friends is to be a friend.

Materials Needed:

- "Call Me When You Need a Friend" activity sheet
- Markers; pencils

Directions:

1. Ask students to tell you things they like about a good friend. Write these on the board. *Responses:* "Listens to me when I'm talking." "Won't tell my secrets." "Fun to be around." "Does things I want, too."

2. Discuss what children say to a friend when a friend tells them about a problem they are having. Discuss together each question below. Responses are given together or individually. Explain that the ideal way to help a friend is found in the last question.

    Do you say, "Hey, it's your problem?" *Response:* "No."

    Do you say you don't know and act like you don't care? *Response:* "No."

    Do you try to help your friends think of ways to solve their problems? *Response:* "Yes."

3. Pass activity sheets to your class. Tell them this is a practice page for helping friends to come to their own solutions for their problems. Decide whether you will read each problem situation and solve it together as a class, in small cooperative group discussions, or individually. Students write the letter of the solution they think is the best one for each problem.

4. *Answers:* A—#2; B—#5; C—#3.

Role-Plays:

Students role-play the problem situations along with the best solutions from the sheet. Students also role-play other ideas for solutions of their own. Choose volunteers to role-play and give them time to rehearse before doing the scenes for the class. Discuss together the solutions role-played after they are performed.

CALL ME WHEN YOU NEED A FRIEND

The best way to have a friend is to *be* a good friend. If your friends have problems, do you help them find ways to solve them? Practice by giving your solutions to the problems below. Write the *number* of the best answer under each problem.

Possible Solutions:

1. Scare your little sister by yelling to her what you'll do to her if she takes your stuff again!

2. Make time to play with your little sister *in your room* and choose one thing she can take to play with and bring back later in perfect shape so she can borrow one more thing.

3. Study an extra 15 minutes Monday to Thursday and get someone to help you with what you don't understand.

4. What can you do? It takes hard work to make good grades. Who wants to work that hard?

5. Join a school sport or club so you can meet kids. Then invite them to your house.

6. Pretend you're sick so you won't feel all alone at school.

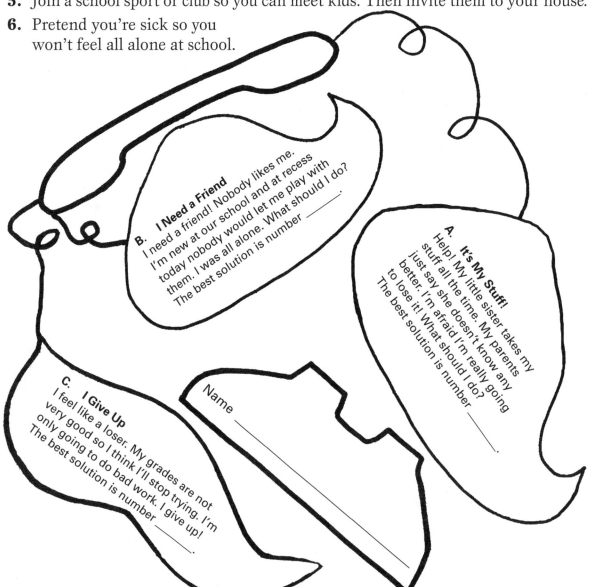

B.   I Need a Friend
I need a friend! Nobody likes me. I'm new at our school and at recess today nobody would let me play with them. I was all alone. What should I do? The best solution is number _____

A.   It's My Stuff!
Help! My little sister takes my stuff all the time. My parents just say she doesn't know any better. I'm afraid I'm really going to lose it! What should I do? The best solution is number _____.

Name _____

C.   I Give Up
I feel like a loser. My grades are not very good so I think I'll stop trying. I'm only going to do bad work. I give up! The best solution is number _____.

2–15. PAINT WITH LOVE

Objective:

Young children each have a turn being brushed with "strokes of love" by their classmates and teacher.

Materials Needed:

- "Paint with Love" activity sheet
- Scissors
- Markers or pens

Directions:

1. This activity is for primary students. It is an opportunity for each student to receive "strokes of love" from classmates. For some students it will leave a lasting positive impression, especially for those who receive few "strokes" outside the school.

2. Students enjoy having their own paintbrushes with their names on them. Paintbrushes may all be hung on a clothesline or on a colorful ladder you make in a corner of the room. Children should sign their names on the paintbrush activity sheets, decorate their paintbrushes, and cut them out. (If you plan to hang them, you may want to add a hole near the top before you copy the sheets.)

3. Students will look forward to your calling everyone together for "paint with love" time. It is up to you how you will choose the child's turn to be painted with love. One idea is to have names in a colorful "paint can" and then draw a name for each "paint with love" session. That way it is not seen as a reward for good work or good behavior. It is important not to withold a child's name for "paint with love" for misbehaving. Perhaps the last two names in the "paint can" could be drawn together so that one child is not left disappointed until the very last name is drawn.

4. In a circle, students take turns giving a "stroke of love" to the student whose name is drawn. He or she stands in the middle of the circle. Children in the circle use their paintbrushes as they pretend to "paint" the child gently while speaking softly with imaginary strokes. As they paint, they should finish the sentence stems "You are . . ." Sentence-stem completions may be: bright, happy, fun, smart, helpful, kind, good, artistic, musical, etc. Students should feel free to offer spontaneous descriptions as long as they are positive. No students may pass or give a put-down. This is rarely an issue as students look forward to this activity and derive almost as much pleasure from watching a classmate receive "strokes" as they do themselves.

5. To add to the drama for the student being stroked, you may want to dim the lights and play a tape the children like. Or your class could sing a song directed to the child in the center. The point is to make the child feel the center of all attention for his or her "paint with love" day!

I would like to acknowledge *Full Esteem Ahead* by Diane Loomans for this idea. (See Read More About It! Section 4.)

PAINT WITH LOVE

Use your special paintbrush to give imaginary paint strokes of love to your class-mates! While you "paint" them, say what is special about them. Take turns so everybody in your class will be brushed with love. Put your name on your paint-brush below and cut it out so when it is your turn, you will have **your own special paintbrush!**

2-16. STARS

Objective:

Children are given the opportunity to give written boosters to friends, letting them know they are special as well as why they shine. The activity provides a lesson in *giving* to others we care about.

Materials Needed:

- "Stars" activity sheet
- Colored pencils or markers
- Yellow bristol board or construction paper
- *Optional:* scissors, paste
- *Optional:* glitter

Directions:

1. Pass out activity sheets to your class. Ask for a volunteer to read orally about the tale of the Starcatcher. After the Starcatcher story is read, tell your children they are all going to be starcatchers for this activity!

2. Ask children if they have friends who brighten up their days when they are sad. *Responses:* "The people who are really my friends help me feel better when I'm down." "A lot of kids are just worried about their own problems. I know I have REAL friends when they take the time to tell me something positive to brighten me up." "A good friend knows how to get my mind off my troubles and onto something totally different—a distraction! It works!" Explain to your class that these friends are valuable. They do not ask for boosters; they *give* because they *care.* It is thoughtful, however, to tell them you appreciate their helping you out when you feel low.

3. Ask a child to read orally the activity directions. Direct your children's attention to the stars on their sheets. Remind them to fill in the name of a special friend. Advise them to give some thought to which special friends they will choose for their stars. When the stars have been completed, the children may then cut out the stars and present them to the recipients! Here are some alternative ideas for presenting the stars:
   - Stars are mounted on yellow bristol board with added wands (for younger students).
   - Personal cards are made from folded colored paper with the stars pasted on the cover. Inside the card, children could include either a poem written to the friends or a personal written recollection of special times in which the friends brightened them up (for older students).
   - Cooperative groups of six children pass activity sheets to one another after children have written their names on their sheets. Each star on each group member's sheet will be filled in with shining qualities others have noticed.

Bulleting Board Link:

The bulletin board caption may read "Here's How We Sparkle!" "Put a Twinkle in Someone's Eyes!" "Our Shining Stars," or "We Glitter in Grade ____." Any of the above uses of the stars may be mounted under one of these captions. For fun and sparkle, add some glitter to the stars!

STARS

There is an old tale about a Starcatcher who wanted to give something special to all her friends. She looked up at the shining stars winking back at her, giving her an idea. The stars lit up the dark sky just as her friends brightened her up when she felt sad. The Starcatcher grinned and whispered a plan, "I'll catch all those sparkling stars and give them to my friends to show them how they brighten my days!"

Do you have friends who brighten your days when you feel sad or lonely? If so, you may not be able to catch any real stars to give them like the Starcatcher did, but you can let them know how much their friendship means to you. In the stars below, fill in the names of three friends. Cut out the stars and give them to your friends.

2–17. JUGGLING FOR JOY

Objectives:

Children learn the meaning of *cooperation* as they play a noncompetitive game in which teamwork is a natural outcome. Everyone emerges as a winner in noncompetitive games.

Materials Needed:

- "Juggling for Joy" activity sheet
- One beanbag for each set of two players (beanbags are preferable to soft balls because balls roll away)

Directions:

1. As a warm-up for the "Juggling for Joy" activity sheet, play a game of cooperative juggling. Discuss safety issues when throwing beanbags such as making eye contact between the thrower and the receiver and calling the person's name, if needed. Tell them that hard or wild throws may cause injury to the eyes.

2. Have children form either one large circle for an older group, or two or three small circles for a younger group or for a large class. Tell them they are going to receive beanbags and that by working together, they will be able to juggle. Children need to remember two things:

    a. Who to throw to

    b. Who throws to them

3. Choose two children to demonstrate throwing and receiving to one another across the circle. The idea is to keep the beanbag moving quickly, concentrating on receiving or throwing to partners only. After assigning partners, pass out a beanbag to one of each pair of partners. Allow partners to stand in two lines and practice throwing and receiving before forming a circle to begin throwing and receiving at the same time. Children will soon discover that each partner needs to concentrate on throwing and receiving with his or her partner only. They will also begin to create a rhythm when everyone throws and receives in a steady flow. If a child drops a beanbag, the game goes on after it is picked up. *Nobody is asked to leave the game for missing a beanbag.* There are no winners or losers in this noncompetitive game.

4. Once children have gotten the idea of the flow of giving and receiving, stop the activity by calling "Freeze in your positions!" Children holding the beanbags throw them into the beanbag container as you call their names.

5. Back in the classroom, pass activity sheets to children. Ask if they can each figure out the message on the juggling balls. Tell them that as they juggled the beanbags with their partners, they needed this message to reach the unity needed to throw and to catch without missing.

6. After children have individually written the message, **cooperation,** ask for a volunteer to write the answer on the board.

7. Direct attention to the bottom of the activity sheet. Ask children to write two things they learned about cooperation during their juggling game. *Possible Responses:* "You need to tune out the distracting noise around you and tune in to your partner." "You should be patient if your partner drops it or doesn't make a great throw or they may get shook up next time." "If you look right at your partner, you throw and catch better." "We called out each other's names every time we threw so we'd be ready!" "We discovered that the underthrow worked the best for us."

8. Have a class follow-up discussion on the importance of cooperation in different areas of our lives such as family, sporting, social, or community charitable events. Ask for examples of times they have had an event that was enhanced by people cooperating. Follow the discussion of cooperation with an event that was dampened by people *not* acting cooperatively.

Name _____

These kids are jumping for joy because they figured out the message on the juggling balls. Can you figure out the message? Write it below.

CLUE: It means working together to play a game or to accomplish something.

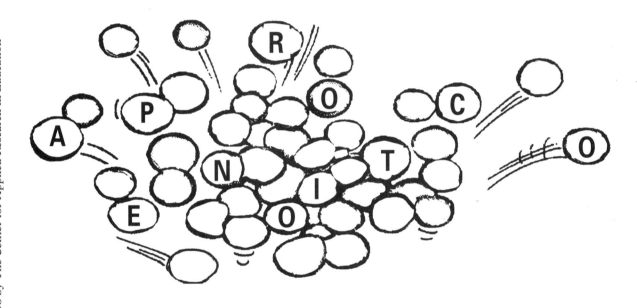

THE MESSAGE IS: _____

Play the JUGGLING GAME! Instead of competing against others, join together to share a fun game. Then write down two things you learned about cooperation in this game:

1. _____

_____

2. _____

_____

2-18. YOU'RE A NACHO ABOVE
2-19. MY LOOT BAG OF GOODIES

Objectives:

Children learn to recognize who are the special people in their lives, why they are special, and the importance of telling them how they are special to them.

Materials Needed:

- "You're a Nacho Above" and "My Loot Bag of Goodies" activity sheets
- *Optional:* basket of nachos, salsa and other Mexican snacks
- *Optional for nachos:* light brown construction paper
- *Optional for sombreros:* colorful bristol board, sequins and yarn
- *Optional for maracas:* dried beans; seeds or large beads; two paper cups; glue, masking tape; colorful tissue paper
- Markers; scissors; assorted colored paper; paste

Directions:

1. Announce to your class that they are going to have a pretend party (or you can have a Mexican celebration and serve real nachos, tortilla chips, or other Mexican snacks, if desired) in which *they can invite three people.* Ask who they would choose to invite. Choose several volunteers to share who they would invite. Then ask what they can say about the people they would like to invite to their party. *Response:* "We like to invite people we care about who are special to us." Most students will choose parents, grandparents, and other relatives, friends, teachers, and coaches.

2. Ask how many students tell the people they chose to invite to the party that they are special and how much they appreciate the special things they do with and for them. Volunteers may share what they do for or say to those special people.

3. Write the term "compliment" on the board. Tell your class they have just been telling you about the compliments they give to others. Ask for synonyms for this term. *Responses:* "Booster." "Something nice." Ask how they feel when others give them compliments. *Responses:* "I feel great!" "I feel like I did something well for them to compliment me. Then I just want to do more because I'm encouraged."

4. Decide which of the above activity sheets you will use first. You may want to use the sheet you do not choose to use now as a reinforcement activity after a couple of months. Both sheets stress the compliments to people special to children.

Art Link for "You're a Nacho Above":

Students enjoy making their own paper sombreros decorated with sequins, glitter and yarn. Slits should be cut inside the sombreros, if desired, for the following cooperative group activity: Children cut out five "nachos" out of posterboard or construction paper, each with their names on the top. Cooperative groups of six children are formed. Children pass their nachos to members of the group to write one positive quality about them. Children receive their five nachos back to place in slits inside their sombreros.

Another activity that children enjoy is making Mexican maracas. They place beads, beans, or seeds in a cup, then turn the second cup upside down and tape on top of the other cup. The newly-formed maracas are then covered with colorful tissue-paper decorations.

Bulletin Board Link:

A fun activity for bulletin boards is to have children decorate a huge sombrero made of posterboard with a large slit inside. Students cut nacho shapes out of brown paper and then write their names at the top with one positive quality about themselves written under their names. All the nachos are then placed in the slit of the sombrero with the caption "Our Class Is a Nacho Above!"

Name _____

YOU'RE A NACHO ABOVE

Think of the people in your life who are special to you. Do you tell them they are special? Do you tell time why they are special? Giving compliments to people we care about is important. In the boxes below, choose three people you want to compliment and what you will say to them.

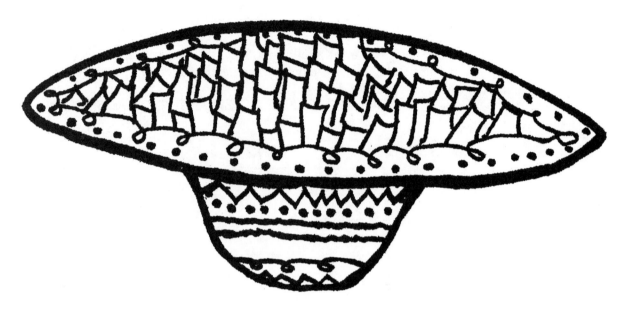

SPECIAL PERSON	COMPLIMENT

MY LOOT BAG OF GOODIES

Write three of your favorite things you like about yourself in three of the candies. Cut them out and paste them into the loot bag. Think of someone special and fill in the other three candies telling him or her the special thing they do that you like. Cut out and paste them to a card you decorate for the special person.

2-20. SURFING THE NET

Objective:

Children learn about differences in cultural backgrounds which helps lead to fewer conflicts as a result of respect and understanding outside their own experiences.

Materials Needed:

- "Surfing the Net" activity sheet
- Notebook and pen for interviews

Directions:

1. Students will recognize Wilbert when you pass out the activity sheets showing Wilbert with his surfboard and tennis racket intending to "surf the net." You may enjoy sharing the humor of Wilbert's latest mix-up when he confuses the terms used for using the Internet.

2. You may want to begin your discussion of the term "culture" with your class by asking what the word means to them. *Response:* "Learning about others' cultures means to find out things about their families, where they came from, their religion, dress, food, and ways of celebrating special days." Call upon volunteers who may enjoy sharing their family backgrounds and customs with the class.

3. After making the point that not all families do things in the same ways—that because of their family backgrounds they often have their own customs—tell children it is interesting for them to get to know these cultures that are different. This activity will enable them to interview three different children at your school or in the community with the parents' supervision (or you may want to confine the interviews to your classroom, especially if you have a culturally diverse class). They should record in a notebook the information they collect during their interviews.

4. Upon completion of the three interviews, students can get further information from the Internet or library about the countries that were the backgrounds for their interviews. This information is then added to their interview notes.

5. Give children a date for the completion of the interviews and computer research. By that date all the information the students have gathered should be neatly copied onto their activity sheets. On the day the activity sheet is due, ask for volunteers to share their interesting stories with the class.

Name _____

SURFING THE NET

Wilbert heard kids talking about finding out where their classmates' families came from. They said they were going to "surf the net" to research the Internet to find information about different *cultures.* Wilbert, confused as usual, got out his tennis racket to take to a tennis net so that he could *surf the net,* too!

Look up information on the Internet about a country you are interested in learning more about. If you don't have access to the Internet, use books from your library. Or ask other kids where their families came from, including new students from other countries, if they agree. Write what you find out.

1. **The country I learned more about was:** _____

2. **Here are interesting things about this country:**

   _____

   _____

   _____

3. **If I visited this country, here are some things I would need to know:**

   Language(s) I'd need to learn: _____

   Weather in July (that's when I would be able to travel there!) _____

   _____

   Some *fun* facts I enjoyed learning: _____

   _____

4. **My source(s) of information:** _____

2–21. STICKY SITUATIONS

Objective:

Children are given the opportunity to solve everyday conflict situations to which they can relate.

Materials Needed:

- "Sticky Situations" activity sheet
- Pens, pencils

Directions:

1. Discuss with your class the times they have had to solve conflicts, although not serious, that involved solutions so that nobody felt like a loser. Explain that another way of referring to conflicts that are not especially serious but do involve someone's feelings being hurt are "sticky situations." Have a class discussion about sticky situations you have all had. Ask students to share how they or someone else solved the situations so anyone's feelings that were hurt felt better as a result of the way the conflict was handled. If the sticky situation ended up with someone still feeling hurt, ask how the solution could have been approached differently. Allot time for volunteers to share their experiences.

2. Depending on the age and maturity of your students, you may choose to read and discuss each "sticky situation" on the activity sheet, discuss the solutions, and then write the solutions together. Older students may complete their solutions individually, then discuss and role-play.

3. Students enjoy making up their own sticky situations for their classmates to solve. They can use the back of the "Sticky Situations" activity sheet.

4. After activity sheets are completed, children will enjoy role-playing the "sticky situations." Choose students whose answers on activity sheets reflect solutions in which everybody wins. Those students may then choose partners to role-play their solutions for the class.

Name _____

STICKY SITUATIONS

When a conflict is hard to handle, we may say it is a "sticky situation." Write below, then role-play how *you* would handle them so that *everybody* in the conflict will feel good about the solution.

1. STICKY SITUATION: "Everybody's Mad at Me!"

Your friend is late to meet you after school to walk home together. It turns out she had to stay after to finish some math. After waiting ten minutes, you start to go home. When you get home, your Mom is annoyed you are late and your friend calls to say she is mad at you for not waiting! You . . .

_____

_____

2. STICKY SITUATION: "Groaner Loaner"

You *loaned* your friend some money ($1.50 to be exact) and now two weeks have gone by and you haven't seen any of that money! You . . .

_____

_____

3. STICKY SITUATION: "Tough Decision"

You just get home from school when your friend calls to invite you over to watch a video you have wanted to see for a long time. But you had *promised* your neighbors to go next door right after school to help *(not* to babysit) with their new baby. You . . .

_____

_____

4. STICKY SITUATION: "Secrets"

You just heard everybody knows about a secret you had told to only one friend. You don't think they could have found out about the secret from anybody else except your friend. You . . .

_____

_____

5. STICKY SITUATION: "Duty Calls"

You and your friend are asked to help with the kindergarten's art project during your recess. Your friend sends a message he can't come. It is a big job by yourself and you had counted on working with your friend. You find out later he was playing soccer at recess. You . . .

_____

_____

2–22. THROW IT OUT!

Objective:

Children realize they sometimes judge others by *outside* factors; they need to focus on getting to know people on the *inside* as they "throw out" their judgments.

Materials Needed:

- "Throw It Out!" activity sheet
- Pens, markers
- *Optional for bulletin board link:* light brown paper; black markers; rope

Directions:

1. Have a discussion with children about how we *think* about people before we get to actually know them. Write the words "different," "prejudice," "judge," "inferior," and "superior" on the board. Ask for a student to tell you what these words have in common. *Response:* "All these words mean when people first see somebody who looks *different* from them, they are *prejudiced* and *judge* them by thinking they are *inferior* or lower than they are. They feel *superior* by putting them down, making fun of them or ignoring them by not letting them join in."

2. Pass activity sheets to your class. Ask children to read each question carefully and to fill out the checklist. After completing the checklist, answer the questions at the bottom of the page.

3. After students have completed their sheets, form cooperative groups to decide upon which situations from the activity sheets they choose to role-play. Students in each group may decide how many situations they will act out. This is followed by each group practicing role-playing the situations on the activity sheet. Students then perform their role-plays for the class.

Bulletin Board Link:

Wilbert's picture with the basketball net (from the activity sheet) is enlarged and displayed. Or a facsimile basketball net could be made with ropes knotted and plastic spiral bindings put together to form a hoop top. Under the net, basketballs made from light brown paper and designed with black markers contain the words each student will be "throwing out." They may choose additional words to those given in the activity above such as "stereotype," "rascism," and other words they use to deal with judging people before getting to know them.

THROW IT OUT!

Sometimes we think *something* about a person before we even get to know that person! Have you judged people by the way they dress, the color of their skin, their weight, or something else *you can see?* What about the things you can't see—like their hearts, what it's like for them at home, what they think about? If you get to know them inside, not just what you see outside, you will be *throwing out your old way* of getting to know people. Differences in people don't mean there have to be conflicts!

What do you think about when you see a person for the first time? Put a check in front of the things you have thought about people when you've only seen them on the *outside:*

1. _____ I think if a person's skin color is different from mine, that person is probably slow to learn.

2. _____ If someone's clothes are too short, dirty or old, I think I'm a little bit better and don't want to be with that person.

3. _____ If another kid is small or fat, I join others who are making fun, saying "shorty" or "fatty."

4. _____ Somebody who doesn't speak English well doesn't really belong with my friends and me.

5. _____ Somebody who dresses in the style of another country should go back to that country!

If you checked off any of the above, *write* below how you would think differently about the person if you look *inside* the person—not just what you see on the outside:

I will think differently for number(s): _____

Here's why: _____

_____

_____

_____

2–23. REAL VALUE

Objective:

Children learn to recognize the importance of the beliefs (values) by which they live.

Materials Needed:

- "Real Value" activity sheet
- Colored markers; crayons

Directions:

1. Write the term "value" on the board. Discuss the meaning with your students. After some class discussion, the following definitions will emerge: "A value is something you choose to do because you believe it is the right thing for you to do in that situation, no matter what others around you are doing. It does not matter if you are the only one who knows what you are doing; you will stand by the value as if thousands of people were watching you."

2. Ask your students for some experiences they have had that tested their values and if they stood by their values. *Response:* "Once at the store I put a bubblegum in my pocket and after I left the store I decided to take it back even though nobody told me to. I knew it was dishonest."

3. Pass activity sheets to your class. Tell them they may choose to write about or to illustrate one time they stood by their values (or three different times they stood by their values).

4. If some students have difficulty with the concept of "value" and cannot think of a value they hold as their own, suggest they do an example of someone they have noticed doing the right thing when faced with a choice between right and wrong.

    Note: If a child has no role model from whom he or she has learned values, a scene from a book or movie or a role model from your school could be given, what the value was, and how the value was upheld.

Alternative Activity:

In each reel students may choose three values they want to hold most strongly and write how they want to uphold those values. *For example:* "I value honesty. I will not look at someone else's work and copy it on tests or for homework." "I value going to my church or synagogue one day every week. I will go when others at home don't go."

Bulletin Board Link:

Display a long "roll of film" unwinding with each frame filled with pictures of people involved in standing by their values. Students choose photos from magazines or newspapers, or make their own illustrations. The (computer-printed) caption is "Here's How We Unwind" or "Lights, Cameras, Action on 'Reel' Values."

REAL VALUE

The frames that make up movie films are also called reels.Now picture this! In the movie reel below, write about a time in your life you felt had *real value* in a lesson you learned. These times helped to make you the person you are today by teaching you **values** you now practice whenever you have to decide between right and wrong. For example, think about times you had to choose to do the *honest* thing when only yourself would know what you did.

My Real Value Lesson

by _____

2–24. PUT YOUR BEST FOOT FORWARD
2–25. MY VALUES COAT OF ARMS

Objective:

Children are taught to stand by their values or beliefs of right and wrong.

Materials Needed:

- "Put Your Best Foot Forward" and "My Values Coat Of Arms" activity sheets
- Pencils; pens

Directions:

1. Form a circle to introduce a class discussion of the term "value." Write the word on the board along with the definitions students give to you during the discussion. *Responses:* "A value is what you stand by no matter what tempts you to do the opposite." "It's what you do you think is right and know nobody else may ever know about it!"

2. Divide your class into small groups to discuss the student-given defintions of "value" as they see it. Appoint one student in each group to take notes on the group discussions and to be prepared to later share them with the class. Choose groups of children so that each feels comfortable to share experiences they have had that tested their values.

3. Decide if you are going to have children complete their activity sheet "problems" that test their values in their small groups or individually. Pass out activity sheets. (#5 gives them the opportunity to share their own real or made-up value-testing story. These may be presented to the members of their small groups and role-played after being discussed together.)

4. As a follow-up to "Put Your Best Foot Forward," distribute "My Values Coat of Arms" activity sheets for students to complete individually. Ask students if they know what a "coat of arms" is. *Response:* "A light garment worn over armor decorated and arranged on a shield with a special emblem of identification." This activity can be compared to shields they wear—their values—that help protect them from doing the wrong thing. Go over the sentence-stem completions together to clarify any questions about values.

Bulletin Board Link:

Display students' values coats of arms in your classroom with the caption "Here's What We Value" or "Our Values Coats of Arms."

Name _____

PUT YOUR BEST FOOT FORWARD

Have you ever said or done something you didn't really want to say or do but did anyway because you didn't want to feel embarrassed with your friends? **Values** are your beliefs of right and wrong that you stand up for no matter what. Below give some examples of values you stand up for.

1. I can put a small item from the corner store in my pocket when nobody sees me. I will . . .

   _____

   _____

2. If a group of my friends makes fun of somebody else and they all start to laugh, I will . . .

   _____

   _____

3. Nobody's home and I have the chance to watch a TV show with a rating I'm not allowed to watch if a grownup is home. I miss lots of shows I want to see! Now I can watch whatever I want and nobody except myself will know. I will . . .

   _____

   _____

4. One of the kids in my group has a cigarette and everybody tries a puff. When it's my turn I . . .

   _____

   _____

5. Here is my own "Put Your Best Foot Forward" story. I'll share it with my classmates so they can see my values.

   _____

   _____

Name _____

MY VALUES COAT OF ARMS

Your *values* are the principles you stand by when choosing what you feel is right and wrong. Fill in the sentence-stem completions inside your Values Coat of Arms. Your answers will reveal the values you hold important.

One thing I do well is . . . _____

Strongest Value I hold is . . . _____

Family value most impressed on me is . . . _____

One valuable thing I want to achieve is . . . _____

The symbol that represents the way I would like others to

think of me is . . . _____

Four words best describing me are . . . _____

_____   _____   _____

Extra Value!!!!

1. Do the values you have learned from your family affect many of the decisions you make when they involve making a choice between right and wrong? Why or why not?

   _____
   _____
   _____
   _____

2. Does the way you would like to be seen by others reflect your *true* values? _____ Why or why not?

   _____
   _____
   _____
   _____

2-26. THE DREAM RANCH
2-27. CLOUDS TO STARS

Objective:

Children are encouraged to dream and to turn their dreams into goals.

Materials Needed:

- "The Dream Ranch" story
- "Clouds to Stars" activity sheet
- *Optional:* glitter or glitter markers, glue

Directions:

1. Have a "dream session" with your children. Make it a relaxing time. If you have carpet in your classroom, ask the children to sit around you as you make yourself comfortable also. Begin by sharing your own dreams with your children.

2. Ask children what some of their dreams are. Listen intently to each child and encourage each of them to dream. Discuss some people in their lives they know, have read, or heard about whose dreams became real. Examples may be sports heroes but should also include everyday people they know.

3. Write the words "dream" and "goal" on the board. Ask students for their own meanings for the word "dream." *Responses:* "Something I hope will come true." "An idea in my mind I want very much." Ask for their meanings of "goal." *Responses:* "I make up my mind to get it!" "I have a purpose to go for." If you ask for their own meanings before giving them the goal-setting steps, the steps will hold more meaning for them.

4. Introduce to students the steps (written on chart or board) they need to turn a dream into a goal:

    Step #1. Write down what it is you want to go for.
    Step #2. Write a date when you will get your goal.
    Step #3. Write who or what you need to do to get your goal.
    Step #4. Picture yourself getting your goal. (Visualize.)
    Step #5. Evaluate every day how you did. Learn from any mistakes and keep on trying!

5. Remind children that if they *aim high* and happen to fall short, they are still much further ahead than they would have been if they had not set high goals!

6. Read "The Dream Ranch" story to students to introduce them to goal setting.

7. Pass out the "Clouds to Stars" activity sheet. Instruct children to write two of their dreams inside the clouds. Then, in the stars, write how they plan (using the five steps above) to turn their dreams into goals.

8. After completing their clouds to stars, children may enjoy decorating the outline of their stars with glitter. Both clouds and stars look colorful with paper clouds mounted on pale blue paper or the stars mounted on gold foil.

Bulletin Board Link:

The bulletin board caption is, "We Do Something About Our Dreams!" Students cut out and display their clouds (mounted on cotton puffs or clouds made of pale blue paper or flannel) and stars (sprinkled with glitter or mounted on gold foil) from activity sheets. Clouds could be hung on the left side of the display under the heading "Our Dreams" and stars hung on the right side under the caption "Our Goals."

THE DREAM RANCH

"The most deadly of all sins is the mutilation of a child's spirit."

—Erik H. Erikson

The class assignment was to write about a goal students wanted to attain when they grew up. Monty enthusiastically worked on his assignment and was pleased with his final product, the dream ranch he wanted to own one day. He drew the plans for every square foot of the ranch house right down to the huge stone fireplace! He wrote passionately about his plans for his ranch and drew the surrounding acres of land and the animals that would graze on those acres. He dreamed of this ranch becoming a reality when he grew up.

He handed in his paper with the other students the next day. Several days later, the papers were handed back to the class and Monty was shocked to see a red "F" at the top of his dream ranch. After class he asked his teacher, "Why did I get an "F" on my dream ranch? I worked hard on the plans for my ranch." The teacher replied, "This is a wonderful ranch. However, it is an unrealistic goal for you. You are the son of an itinerant farmer and this ranch, all this land, and all these animals would cost a lot of money. It is unlikely you would ever be able to afford this ranch. But you put a lot of effort into the assignment so I'll give you another opportunity to re-write your paper and I will erase this "F" and give you a new grade."

Monty went home and asked his dad what he should do about his assignment. His dad told him, "Son, I can't tell you what to do this time. But I do think the decision you make will significantly affect your future." Monty knew what he would do. At school the next day, he approached his teacher and handed him back his dream ranch story. He said to his teacher, "You keep this 'F' and I'll keep my dream." Monty walked away with his head held high.

Years later, the same teacher took his inner city students on a trip to a beautiful ranch. His students noticed a big stone fireplace with an unusual wall hanging above it. It was a story written in childish handwriting and a detailed ranch house, land and animals. It was the ranch they had just toured! It also had a big red "F" at the top of the page. The teacher went over to the owner of the ranch, Monty Roberts, who had opened up his ranch for inner city children to visit. He recognized him as the boy whom he had taught many years before who had turned in an assignment on a dream ranch.

The teacher looked at Monty and said, "Monty, years ago I stole a lot of dreams. I'm so glad you held on to your dream, made it a goal and got it!"

—Monty Robert's Story, *Chicken Soup for the Soul* by Jack Canfield and Mark V. Hansen. Health Communications, 1993. Used with permission.

Name _____

CLOUDS TO STARS

Be sure to dream! Then turn the dreams into goals so you can make your dreams come true. *Example:* **Dream in Cloud:** "I'd like to be good in Math." **Goal in Star:** "I will work an extra 15 minutes on Math every weekday and raise my Math grade to a "B" by my next report card." Write your dreams in the clouds below. Then write in the stars your goals of how you will make your dreams come true.

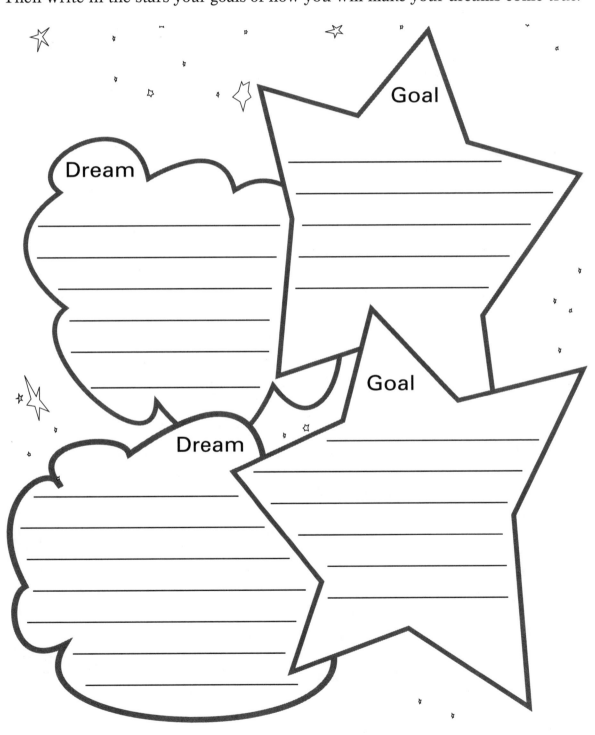

COMPUTE YOUR GOALS

Step 1. Decide *what you want to do or reach* and make it your GOAL. For example, you may want a new headset. What will you do to reach your goal?

Step 2. Make sure your goal is *realistic*. It may be a bit out of reach but it must be something you *can* reach. Don't get in over your head.

Step 3. There are two types of goals: *long-term goals,* like graduating from high school, and *short-term goals,* like improving your next report card by bringing each grade up one letter.

Step 4. Moving toward your goal is like climbing a ladder. You want to get to the top of the ladder, but to get there you have to *climb one step at a time.*

Step 5. The most important thing you can do to reach your goal is to *write it out.*

Step 6. Your goal is where you are headed but you will never get anywhere unless you have *a plan* to get there

Step 7. Set *specific* goals you can *measure.* If your goal is to become a better reader, write out how much extra time you will spend each day to improve your reading. Will it be 15 minutes every weekday? Don't just say, "I'm going to read more." You won't be able to measure whether you are moving towards your goal.

Step 8. Cut out an illustration or draw yourself reaching your goal so that you have *a picture in your mind.* Remember, YOU CAN IF YOU BELIEVE YOU CAN!

Step 9. Nobody reaches his or her goal magically. Ask yourself daily, Am I really working hard to reach my goal?"

Step 10. *Write down* what you do that gets you closer to your goal. Don't worry if you make some mistakes. Learn from your mistakes by asking yourself what you are going to change to make sure the same problem doesn't come up again.

Step 11. Share your goals with friends who also have goals so you can encourage each other.

Step 12. Remember, setting goals will help you become the very best person you can be. Reach for the top of your abilities!

HOW DO YOU COMPUTE?

Do you have some good ideas you would like to achieve? Write three of your good ideas below. choose one of them to turn into a goal. Put a check in front of the number you choose.

1. _____

2. _____

3. _____

Now get real about your goal by asking yourself if you will be able to reach it. Make sure you can check out your progress. On the lines corresponding to the letters below, answer the following questions:

A. What do you want to achieve?

B. By when do you plan to achieve it?

C. What or whom do you need to help you achieve it?

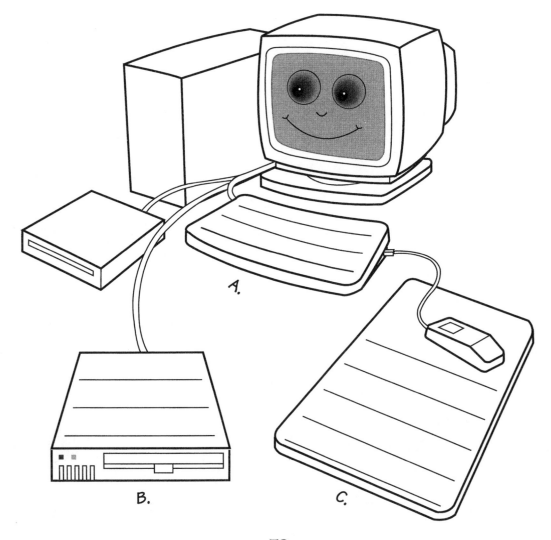

3
Conflict-Resolution Activities for Your Classroom

"I really bonded with the kids. I was teaching from the heart, and the kids' biggest need seemed to be a teacher who cared about them and their individual needs."

Ennis Cosby, Special Education teacher

3–1. DIRECTIONS FOR THE CONFLICT-SOLVING QUIZ

This quiz may be used as a pre-test before Conflict Solving is introduced in your classroom. After you feel your students have completed a sufficient number of conflict-resolution activities, the quiz may again be given and the results compared with the pre-test. Below are the conflict-solving components you are assessing. If a student answer differs from the answer key below, it may be an indicator of weakness in that component and you will know specifically what his or her needs are.

Conflict-Solving Skills to Be Developed in Students:

- **Control of Anger:** able to stop and cool down
- **Collaborative Conflict Solving:** both win; nobody is a *loser*
- **Problem Solving:** able to identify the problem, to brainstorm several solutions, and to choose one that meets needs of both
- **Active Listening:** able to listen to the feelings and needs of the other person involved in the conflict and to repeat back his/her words to him/her
- **Peace Contribution:** feels he or she makes a difference to peace in own school and community

Answer Key:

1. NO; Control of Anger
2. NO; Collaborative Conflict Solving
3. NO; all areas
4. YES; all areas
5. YES; Collaborative Conflict Solving
6. NO; all areas
7. YES; Peace Contribution
8. YES; Control of Anger
9. YES; all areas
10. NO; Control of Anger

Teacher Evaluation—Notes on Weak Areas:

Student:_____   Date: _____

Observed behavior in the area of: _____

My plan to help strengthen that area: _____

_____

_____

Name _____   Date _____

STUDENT CONFLICT-SOLVING QUIZ

Directions: Circle YES or NO depending how you *usually* feel about the statement. Your answers will not be shared with the rest of the class.

YES   NO   **1.** When I am angry, the *anger controls* me.

YES   NO   **2.** I have to win when I have a conflict with someone.

YES   NO   **3.** I use physical force to get my way.

YES   NO   **4.** It is important to me how the other person sees the problem in a conflict with me.

YES   NO   **5.** I think *both* of us should feel like winners after we have solved a conflict together.

YES   NO   **6.** Shouting when I'm angry is the best way to get what I want.

YES   NO   **7.** I can make a difference to world peace even if I'm only one person.

YES   NO   **8.** If I stop to calm down when I'm angry, I can plan what to do next.

YES   NO   **9.** Conflict is a part of my life, so it's helpful to know how to solve our problems so that *nobody feels like a loser.*

YES   NO   **10.** When I'm angry, I tell the person off right away.

Why I answered YES of NO on number(s):

_____

_____

_____

_____

_____

_____

Here are my ideas for solving conflicts so nobody ends up feeling like a loser.

_____

_____

_____

_____

_____

_____

© 1998 by The Center for Applied Research in Education

3–2. ROLLER COASTER DAYS
3–3. CAN YOU CRACK THIS CASE?
3–4. COLOR ME
3–5. COLOR MY FEELINGS

Objective:

Children get in touch with the ups and downs of their feelings.

Materials Needed:

- "Roller Coaster Days" "Can You Crack This Case?" "Color Me" and "Color My Feelings" activity sheets
- Colored pencils, crayons

Directions:

1. Introduce any of these activities by asking how many students have the same feelings every day. From their responses (which will be very few) if any who have the same feelings daily, you may lead into the discussion of how feelings change day to day. Explain that others' feelings often influence our own feelings either negatively or positively.

    For example, point out that a parent who is very tired at the end of a long day of work may be feeling less patient than on other days. He or she might say or do things that might result in the child feeling "down" also. The next day the feelings may be reversed and the parent and child may both feel "up" and enjoy activities together. Ask for volunteers to describe some "up" and "down" experiences they have had lately and some words they could use to sum up those days. *Responses:* "Depressed." "Mad." "Happy." "Awesome!" "Hurt." "Lonely." List the responses on the board as they are given to you so that all the children will see that they all share feelings that go up and down.

2. Pass out "Roller Coaster Days" activity sheets to your class. If desired, explain to older students that a metaphor compares one thing to another. In this activity Wilbert (the recurring comic figure in this book) riding a roller coaster is a metaphor for the "roller coaster" of feelings they "ride" every day. Ask for volunteers to name some things that contribute to positive and negative feelings as you record them on the board.

3. Tell children that they will be like Wilbert riding the roller coaster, describing their feelings every day for one week by filling in words and, if desired, faces describing happy, mad, and sad feelings. Explain that they will be having many different feelings each day but to try to limit their descriptive words (and faces) to only one or two each day and, at the end of the week, they will draw a roller coaster showing the ups and downs for each day of that week.

4. At the end of the week, ask students to evaluate how their week looked as if it were a roller coaster. Ask your class if anybody had a roller coaster that went straight, with no ups and downs. (Responses will be few, if any.) Be sure to look at all roller coasters and

be attentive to any that are "down" each day of the week. If so, you will want to have some private time with the child to see if the "down" week was an aberration or if there is a problem. You may want to have the child do more roller coasters for the next few weeks, telling him or her that you will be the only one to see them.

Explain that it is natural to have good and bad, mad and sad days and that very few people, if any, have the same daily feelings over and over, although some very sad people with problems may have these "down" feelings daily until they work through their problems. You may choose to have volunteers draw their roller coasters on the board so that children will see they are alike in their feelings that go up and down.

5. As a follow-up activity, give "Can You Crack This Case?" activity sheets to students. They will see Wilbert has dropped the peanut jar and needs help cracking his case of the scrambled letters. Beside each peanut is a word to be unscrambled. Students are to write on each numbered line the word they unscramble so that a message is formed. The mixed-up message is: **"Our feelings go up and down."**

Give students the opportunity to write on the back of the activity sheet about the "My Roller Coaster Day" or "My Nutty Up and Down Day" they have had when their feelings went up and down. When they are completed, ask for volunteers to share their stories with the class. You may want to write about one of your own "roller coaster days"! Children will then realize we all have good and bad days!

6. Pass the "Color Me" activity sheet to primary students. Use the same directions as above but modified for younger students. Students color the pencils the colors given to "happy" or yellow, "sad" or blue, and "mad" or red for each day of the school week. Choose a quiet time in the afternoon for children to fill in their colors for that day. Tell them to try to think of all the feelings they had that day and to sum them all up or to put them all together into one color. Then one happy, sad, or mad face is drawn in boxes at the bottom of the sheet for each day.

As a follow-up to "Color Me" pass "Color My Feelings" activity sheets to children to write or dictate to you things that make them happy, sad, or mad. If you have a class discussion with volunteers sharing what they wrote on their activity sheets, children will realize they all share similar happy, sad, and mad feelings.

Name _____

ROLLER COASTER DAYS

Do you feel happy some days and mad or sad other days? Feelings are like a roller coaster going up and down. Choose one word to describe your feelings each day for one week. At the end of the week, draw a roller coaster describing your week.

Monday	Tuesday	Wednesday	Thursday	Friday	Saturday	Sunday

My Roller Coaster for the Week Looks like This:

CAN YOU CRACK THIS CASE?

Wilbert is GOING NUTTY trying to crack the mystery of the words next to the peanuts when they fell out of their jar. Unscramble the word beside each peanut and write it below.

1. _____

2. _____

3. _____

4. _____

5. _____

6. _____

I've cracked a nutty case! I put all the words together and here is the sentence I unscrambled:

_____

_____

_____

On the back of this page, write about a day when your feelings went up and down.

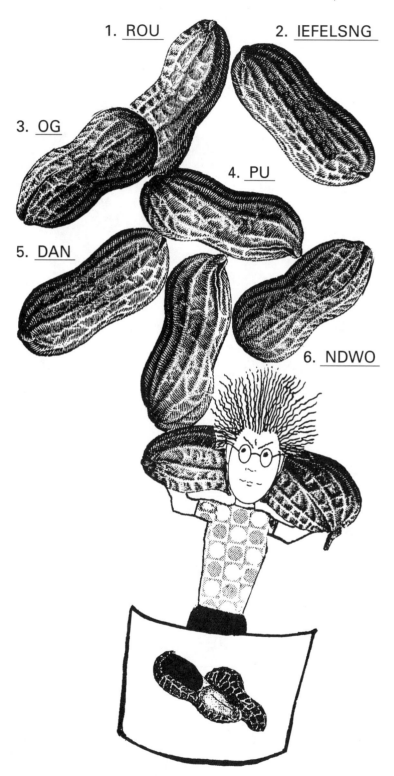

1. ROU

2. IEFELSNG

3. OG

4. PU

5. DAN

6. NDWO

Name _____

COLOR ME ...

Color the pencil yellow, blue, or red every day of the week. Put a face in the box every day showing your feelings.

Happy—Yellow   **Sad—Blue**   **Mad—Red**

Monday	Tuesday	Wednesday	Thursday	Friday

81

COLOR MY FEELINGS

Write about your feelings in the crayon.

_____ makes me feel happy.

_____ makes me feel sad.

Name _____

Other times I feel

_____

_____

_____

_____

_____

3–6. WINDOWS OF FEELINGS
3–7. KEY TO MY FEELINGS
3–8. WILBERT'S "MANY MOODS" STICK PUPPETS

Objective:

Children identify the different feelings they experience and how they handle them.

Materials Needed:

- "Windows of Feelings" activity sheet
- "Key to My Feelings" activity sheet
- Wilbert's "Many Moods" stick puppets

Directions:

1. Have a class discussion about feelings. Ask children to volunteer the different feelings they experience in one day and how they handle those feelings. Write them on the board as children give them to you. *Response:* "Yesterday I saw this big kid who lives down the street from me coming toward my house. He has bullied me before so *I felt afraid.*" (The word "afraid" is written on the board.) "*I handled it by* looking at him directly in the eye like I wasn't afraid and then I got on my bike and rode down the street." (Write this on the board.)

2. Pass "Windows of Feelings" activity sheets to your class. Ask for a volunteer to read the top of the page. Tell children to write four feelings they have had that day with their faces showing how they feel in the windows.

3. After sheets are completed, discuss together all the different feelings children described in their windows. Ask for volunteers to share their feelings as you write their words on the board or chart. In this way, children will see that others have feelings of sadness, fear, embarrassment, joy, excitement, and other feelings just like they do. They feel more at ease knowing their feelings go up and down just like other children's do.

4. You may use the Wilbert "many moods" stick puppets for student volunteers to hold up as they play the role of Wilbert giving advice to the children about handling their feelings in their windows. A child volunteers a feeling he or she wrote that causes the most concern.

    Example: A child writes "sad" in a window. Ask for a volunteer. "What might our character, Wilbert, say for the child to do about sad feelings?" The volunteer pretends to be Wilbert's Sad Stick Puppet and makes up an answer that will help the child who wrote "sad" on the page. "Last time *I felt sad* because all my friends were busy when I called them. *I handled it by* crying in my room. I didn't handle it very well and next time I'll make plans ahead of time. Next time I'll apologize if I did something wrong to someone, or broke a rule instead of pouting in my room when I get in trouble and waste the whole day there."

5. You may process other children's feelings in their window with a Wilbert stick puppet giving more advice.

6. Pass "Key to My Feelings" activity sheets for students to write about how they handle their feelings.

Bulletin Board Link:

Make a large door with windows for each of the feelings given by the children on their activity sheets. Place a letter on each of the feelings and mark the keys with their corresponding letters. *Example:* **Window:** A. Embarrassed. **Key:** A. I remembered nobody can make me feel low if I don't let them. Use "Key to My Feelings" activity sheet for students to display their best ways of handling their feelings. The keys could be hung on a binder ring. If you have a large number of keys, hang them in small groups in binder rings with string or yarn attached to the keys. The caption is "Doorway to Our Feelings" or "The Keys to Handling Our Feelings."

WINDOWS OF FEELINGS

Think about all the different feelings you have in just one day. Do you feel SAD, MAD, HAPPY, FUNNY, AFRAID and other feelings?

Write four of the feelings you have in one day in the four windows below. Cut out and paste how your face looks when you have that feeling.

KEY TO MY FEELINGS

Write your best ways to handle your feelings when you feel sad or mad.

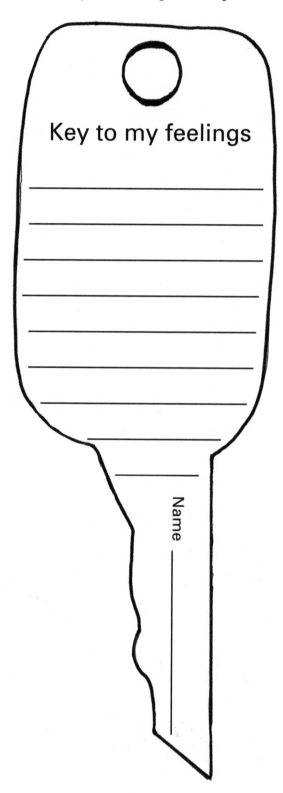

Key to my feelings

Name

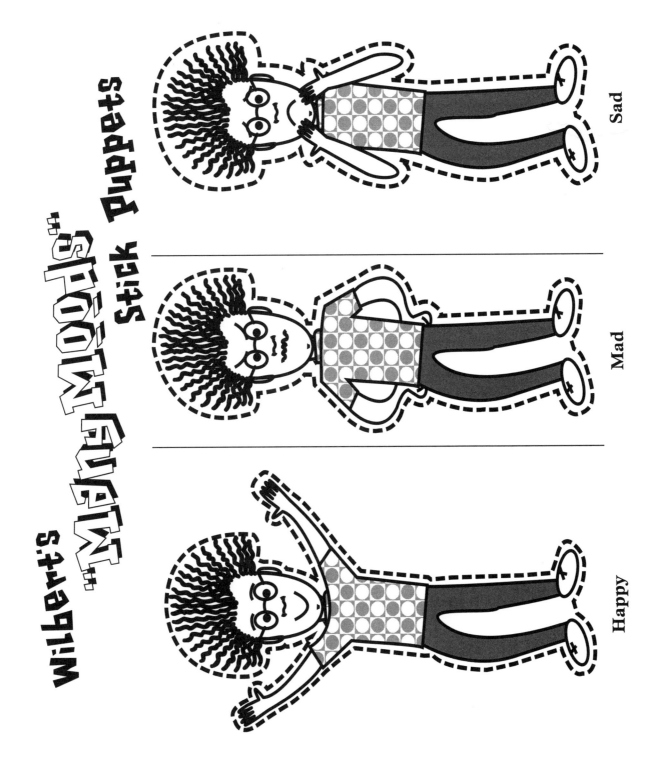

Wilbert's "May Moods" Stick Puppets

Sad

Mad

Happy

3–9. MY BUTTERFLY BOOK OF FEELINGS

Objective:

Primary children "open up" to the variety of feelings they experience every day for several days.

Materials Needed:

- "My Butterfly Book of Feelings" activity sheet
- Yarn to attach pages of book
- Colored markers; pencils; glitter; stickers to decorate pages of book

Directions:

1. Hold an informal circle talk with your students about their *feelings*. Begin by asking how they felt that morning. Try to relate their feelings to events that previously occurred. Take children through the previous day and ask them to relate the different feelings they had at various times throughout the day. Write the words on the board as they give them to you. *Responses:* "I felt . . . sad, mad, happy, afraid, embarrassed, lonely, or scared." Be prepared for some feelings to be described by children without their knowing the term used for the feeling. For example, a child may say she feels upset because she was not helping her dad with the dishes while she was playing with her friend. Explain this is a common feeling we sometimes have when we feel we *should* be doing something instead of what we are choosing to do. You may write the term "guilty" on the board.

2. Explain during your circle talk that it is important for children to identify their feelings as they experience them. Tell children they will keep track of their day-to-day feelings with the butterfly.

3. Pass the "My Butterfly Book of Feelings" activity sheet to your students. If you copy five pages per student, they can keep track of their feelings daily for the school week.

4. Children will enjoy decorating their book pages with glitter, stickers, etc. Children's feelings are written or drawn on each page for the number of days you decide upon. If you decide to make books for each child at the end of the days you specify, attach the pages with colored yarn. Pages with no lines are useful for students who are having difficulty writing or expressing their feelings in writing.

Around-the-Room Link:

Cut out several paper butterflies and in large letters identify the feelings mentioned above—SAD, MAD, HAPPY, AFRAID, EMBARRASSED, LONELY, SCARED, GUILTY—as well as others described by children. Laminate and display the butterflies in the classroom so that students are constantly exposed to the names for the different feelings they are experiencing. If you have difficulty communicating with some of your children about their feelings, ask them to point to the butterfly that expresses how they are feeling at that time. This can be your visual aid in encouraging them to open up to feelings they have difficulty expressing.

MY BUTTERFLY BOOK OF FEELINGS

Name _____ Day of Week _____

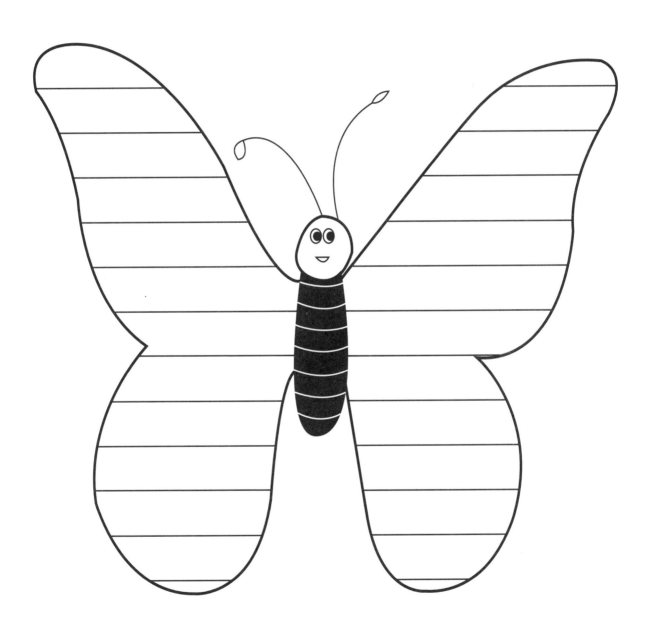

3-10. STORMY AND SMILEY

Objective:

Children self-express feelings while enjoying creating similes.

Materials Needed:

- "Stormy and Smiley" activity sheet
- *Optional:* books on display with examples of similes
- Colored pencils

Directions:

1. Write the term "simile" on the board. Explain that a *simile* is a figure of speech in which one thing is likened to another and that a clue as to whether a comparison is a simile or not is use of the words "like" or "as."

2. Write the following sentence on the board as an example of a simile:

   "Today I feel as warm as sunshine."

   Ask a volunteer to go to the board to underline the clues that tells you it is a simile. (The volunteer should underline the words "as.")

3. Ask students to picture in their minds what stormy clouds look like if they compared them to a person's feelings. Pausing for a moment while they picture simple given objects helps them to form the imagery to create similes and prepares them for other visualization activities. After the pause, ask for volunteers to share what they pictured. *Response:* "I pictured dark clouds that looked mad." Then ask students to form a simile comparing their *angry feelings* to stormy clouds and to thunder using "like" or "as." *Responses:* "I feel *as* angry *as* a stormy cloud." "I feel so mad I'm going to be roaring *like* thunder any minute!"

4. Continue to use the "stormy clouds" example and ask students to now compare their *sad feelings* to the stormy clouds and to create a simile. *Response:* "I feel *as* sad *as* a stormy cloud getting ready to pour my tears all over the earth."

5. Pass the "Stormy and Smiley" activity sheets to the children. Tell children to enjoy making up their own stormy and smiley similes for this activity.

6. After activity sheets have been completed, ask for volunteers to share their favorite similes with the class. Allow plenty of time as children will be happy as larks hearing their classmates' similes as well as sharing their own!

Language Arts Bulletin Board Link:

Display children's favorite similes, along with their illustrations, if desired, with the caption "Our Stormy and Smiley Similes" or "Our Feelings."

Name _____

STORMY AND SMILEY

"I'M BUSY AS A BEE." "HIS TEARS FLOWED LIKE A WATERFALL." When we compare one unlike thing to another by use of words such as "like" or "as," we have created a **simile**. Make up your own similes comparing your feelings to something using *like* or *as*.

Stormy Similes

Make up stormy similes to describe your mad or moody feelings.

1. I can get as mad *as* a (an) _____

2. When I keep my anger hidden I feel as sneaky *as* _____

3. My anger sometimes feels *like* _____

4. Sometimes my moods are as changing *as* _____

5. When I'm really upset by the past and not what's happening now, I feel haunted *like* _____

  ## Smiley Similes

Make up smiling similes that make you feel peaceful and happy.

1. In a conflict my reason usually takes over *like* _____

2. Sometimes I feel peaceful *as* _____

3. When everything is going well I feel *like* _____

4. When I help someone I feel proud *as* _____

5. My happiness feels *like* _____

3–11. STEAMED SCENE

Objective:

Children learn it is natural to have angry feelings; however, it is not acceptable to express angry feelings so that the result is hurting someone else or oneself physically or verbally.

Materials Needed:

- "Steamed Scene" activity sheet
- Colored pencils, crayons or markers

Directions:

1. Ask students to discuss some physical symptoms they notice about themselves when they get angry. *Responses:* "My hands get sweaty." "My stomach hurts." "My mouth feels dry." "My face gets red and feels hot like it's steaming!"

2. Ask students if any of them have ever felt so angry that they were "steaming." *Response:* Most hands will probably go up. Explain that it is natural to feel angry; however, it is not acceptable to hurt themselves or someone else either physically or verbally if they lose their tempers because they don't stop to cool down.

3. Pass the "Steamed Scene" activity sheet to your class for them to write about or illustrate a scenario in which they felt very angry. The questions at the bottom of the page provide the opportunity for them to evaluate how they handled the situation and whether or not they hurt themselves or someone else physically or emotionally. They have the opportunity to then decide what they would do differently in the scenario so that nobody feels like a loser.

   Note: Some children may feel reluctant to reveal a personal steamed scenario. Alternatively, they could choose to make up a scenario to write about or illustrate on their activity sheets.

4. After activity sheets are completed, ask for volunteers to role-play their scenarios. They should be prepared to share the answers to the questions, asking them to evaluate how they handled the conflict and what, if needed, they would do differently next time.

STEAMED SCENE

First write about or draw, then role-play a time you were so angry that you were *steamed!*

_____

_____

_____

_____

_____

_____

_____

_____

_____

_____

Did anybody in this conflict end up feeling like a loser? _____

If so, who? _____ Would you

do anything differently in this conflict? _____ If so,

what? _____

_____

3-12. HOT BBQ SIZZLER—TLC RECIPE

Objective:

Children are given an easy way to remember some guidelines for handling a conflict in a way that nobody ends up feeling like a *loser*. The **BBQ Technique** and the **TLC Recipe** give children the ingredients needed to emerge from the conflict feeling as if the needs of both have been met so that everyone feels happy with the outcome.

Materials Needed:

- "Hot BBQ Sizzler—TLC Recipe" activity sheet
- Scissors
- *Optional:* props for role plays (chef's hat, apron, cooking utensils, portable chalkboard for use as menu)

Directions:

1. Announce to your class that you have a great recipe for them to try, one easy enough for all to have great success. The "fixings" are readily available to each one of them; they all have the ingredients within themselves. They don't even have to go out and buy anything for this recipe! Pass out the activity sheets and choose a student to read aloud the TLC introductory recipe at the top of the sheet.

2. Introduce the **BBQ Technique** and the **TLC Recipe** by writing both on a "menu" chart or board. Explain as you write out the BBQ Technique that these initials (BBQ) serve as a sizzling way to remember **Better Be Quiet** when first facing a conflict situation in which one feels very angry. This technique gives those involved in the conflict time to cool down and to plan how best to proceed. Taking a deep breath and counting to at least ten enables them to control their anger before it controls them. Hold a class discussion about conflicts they have had (volunteers only in order to avoid any embarrassing displays of anger a student would prefer not to disclose in front of classmates) in which they felt their anger controlled them. Ask, "If you had stopped quietly to cool down first, might you have handled your anger more effectively?" *Response:* "I was so mad, I didn't stop to think ahead. I just blurted out some angry shouting and started punching!" Ask if they feel the BBQ Technique would have changed the way the conflict was handled. *Response:* "If I had cooled off, I would not have said and done the things I did that hurt the other person."

3. Give students the ingredients that come after the BBQ Technique, the **TLC Recipe**. Write on your "menu" as you explain each letter of the recipe.

   T: **Tune** in to *both* of your feelings by each taking turns telling your side of the problem.

   L: **Listen** to how the other person sees the problem, then take turns repeating back the other's words.

   C: **Choose a solution** to meet *both* persons' needs so both feel like winners.

Discuss each of the above points by doing some examples of conflict situations given to you by students (real or imagined) and go through the conflict using each of the steps above.

4. After passing out the activity sheets, ask students to think of a real or made-up conflict situation they would like to role-play with a partner. Their lines for the role-play are to be written after each of the TLC letters, following the guidelines for each letter as given in the TLC Recipe.

5. Students may cut out their TLC Recipes to tape to their notebooks for easy reference. You may want to leave your "menu" on display during your Conflict Resolution unit until the students have internalized the desired behavior during conflicts.

HOT SIZZLER!!

Here's a SIZZLER: When a conflict gets "too hot to handle," first remember the **BBQ** technique: Better Be Quiet! Count at least to ten! Then follow this recipe: Don't try to be a hot dog when you find yourself in a pickle. Relish the care you give, turn over gently so nobody gets burned, hold the HOT stuff, and top with TLC (Tender Loving Care)! Grate! Remember to use a little "tenderizer" to soften your conflict by following the **TLC Recipe** below. Then you can say to yourself, "Well done!"

Role-play a conflict situation (real or made-up) with a partner. First, act out how you will use the **BBQ Technique** to cool off. Then role-play using the **TLC Recipe** to solve your conflict.

TLC RECIPE

TUNE IN to both of your feelings by each taking turns telling your side of the problem.

LISTEN to how the other sees the problem, then take turns repeating back the other's words.

CHOOSE A SOLUTION to meet both persons' needs so both feel like winners.

3–13. BRUSH UP ON TLC
3–14. BRUSH IT OFF? NO WAY!

Objective:

Children will *brush up* on the **TLC Recipe**. They are encouraged to describe how they will approach a conflict using the **BBQ (Better Be Quiet) Technique** to calm down, then the **TLC Recipe** to solve the conflict.

Materials Needed:

- "Brush Up on TLC" and "Brush It Off? No Way!" activity sheets
- Colored pencils; markers

Directions:

1. Announce to your students that they are going to receive a tube of Truthpaste (on paper!) for this activity so that they can brush up on their BBQ Technique and TLC Recipe for handling their conflicts. Explain that the Truthpaste is to remind them to *stick to an honest approach* when telling the other person their feelings and their needs.

2. Pass out both activity sheets. Ask for a student volunteer to orally read the activity directions at the top of the activity sheet, "Brush Up on TLC." Students refer to their [Brush It Off? No Way!" activity sheets and read together the story about Perly White's dilemma. Ask students to fill in on their "Brush Up on TLC" activity sheets the solution they would use to solve Perly White's toothpaste problem. They place their solutions in each of the T-L-C letters on the sheet.

3. Students will enjoy using this story as a humorous role-play to act out. Or students could use the idea of this story for their own stories they write about a humorous problem situation they create or one they have experienced. Students then write out the stories and, if desired, role-play for the class.

BRUSH UP ON TLC

Remember to first cool off with the **BBQ Technique** (Better Be Quiet) and the use the **TLC Recipe: T**une in to both of your feelings by each taking turns telling your side of the story. **L**isten to how the other sees the problem, then take turns repeating back the other's words. **C**hoose a solution to meet both person's needs so both feel like winners. Don't give the other person the *brush-off!*

Think of a conflict you are now having in your life—or use the story of Perly White. Write beside each TLC letter written with Truthpaste (be honest!) how you will approach your conflict. Then give yourself some "Way to go, (your name)!" positive strokes!

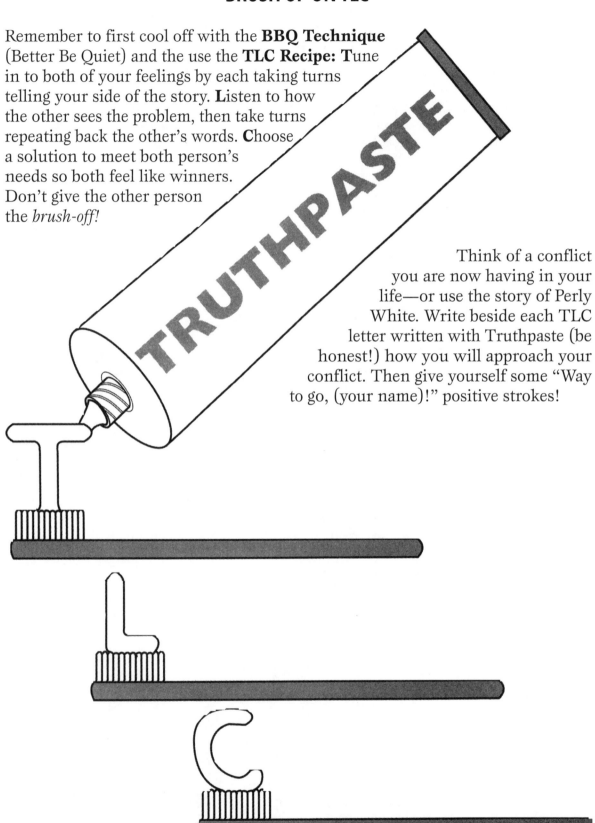

Name _____

BRUSH IT OFF? NO WAY!

Hi, my name's Perly White and here's the situation: My family has different opinions on how to squeeze our toothpaste, which six people share, supposedly, two or three times a day. We're just about split on how to squeeze the tube. Half of our family members squeeze the tube from the middle or even from the top so they can quickly get the toothpaste out, put it onto the toothbrush, and then hurry off. The other family members take the time to squeeze the tube from the bottom, like civilized people, rolling the bottom up as the tube is gradually emptied, which seems to me to be the practical thing to do, even though it may take an extra nine seconds or so.

The same people who squeeze from the bottom also take the time to clean the toothpaste off the top of the tube so it doesn't get goopy! Guess which ones don't put the cap on when they're finished? You guessed it, the middle-of-the-tube squeezers! I usually try to *cap* my annoyance at what to me is an extremely lazy approach by those who don't care when the tube starts to look like a twisty toy. Do you have an issue like this in your family? Maybe you can brush it off better than I can. How would *you* solve this, although small, conflict which is still *really annoying* to a neat person?

Directions:

Use the above story to fill out your "Brush Up on TLC" activity sheet. Go through the problems this family has with their toothpaste using the TLC Recipe. This story may give you a "stroke of genius" for a fun story you could write about a similar ordinary problem you have. *Brush up* on your dramatic role-playing skills using your own similar humorous problem situations and stories (real or made-up) describing how to come up with solutions.

3–15. SMART SIGNALS

Objective:

A plan students can easily remember when they are *so angry that they see RED* is the **Traffic Signal Strategy**. This method enables them to remember steps to take to cool down when their behavior is a *signal* to them that their anger is getting out of hand!

Materials Needed:

- "Smart Signals" activity sheet
- Colored pencils, markers or crayons
- Large traffic light drawn on a chart or the board with strategies for cooling down

Directions:

1. Pass out the activity sheets. Tell students that if they sometimes get so angry that their faces turn red, we use the phrase, "He (or she) sees red!" Ask for a show of hands as to who has ever felt that they were seeing red. *Responses:* Most hands will probably go up. Remind them that anger is a natural emotion everyone feels at times; it is only when anger controls us rather than our controlling the anger that it is a *signal* we need to cool down.

2. Announce to your class that, speaking of signals, there is an easy method they can use the next time their anger makes them feel like they are "seeing red." It is called the **Traffic Signal Strategy**. Ask for volunteers to read the points written beside the traffic light on the activity sheet.

3. Direct students' attention to the conflict quotations at the bottom of the activity sheet. They are to decide which color of the stoplight should be used for each problem and to then write the stoplight color on the lines before each number. On the line under each conflict quotation, they are to decide what the kids in conflict should say *after* they have used the traffic signal strategies. They may create their own conflict situations for #5 and then write which traffic light is needed to help resolve the conflict.

4. Proceed as an individual or as an oral whole-class activity. If done individually, discussion should be held after students have completed the five questions. Students may then share the next step—what the kids in the conflict situations should say next to resolve the conflict. Tell students there are no single responses to each situation; if their responses "work"—that is, if they accomplish cooling down so that they can then plan to solve the conflict so that everyone feels like a winner—then they have used the Traffic Signal Strategy well!

Name _____

SMART SIGNALS

When you find yourself so angry that you "see red"—STOP! Use the **Traffic Signal Strategy**. Follow these signals:

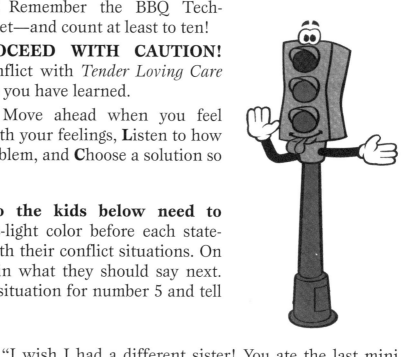

> **Red Light—STOP!** Remember the BBQ Technique—Better Be Quiet—and count at least to ten!
>
> **Yellow Light—PROCEED WITH CAUTION!** Plan to solve the conflict with *Tender Loving Care* using the TLC Recipe you have learned.
>
> **Green Light—GO!** Move ahead when you feel calmer, **T**une in to both your feelings, **L**isten to how the other sees the problem, and **C**hoose a solution so everyone is a winner!

Which traffic light do the kids below need to use? Write in the traffic-light color before each statement to help them out with their conflict situations. On the line under each, fill in what they should say next. Create your own conflict situation for number 5 and tell what you would say next.

1. _____ "I wish I had a different sister! You ate the last mini pizza! You also ate the other three!"

_____

2. _____ "I was really ticked off at you until you explained what happened to the baseball mitt I let you borrow."

_____

3. _____ "Now I'm planning what to do. I almost just quit this team because the coach is always on my case."

_____

4. _____ "I'll make you sorry you ever said that about my skin color!"

_____

5. _____ _____

_____

3–16. I'M A HIT!

Objective:

Primary children learn to focus on how they have handled their angry feelings in the past and positive ways of handling it the next time they have a conflict.

Materials Needed:

- "I'm a Hit!" activity sheet
- Pencils; scissors; brown markers or crayons

Directions:

1. Have a discussion with children about anger. Make the point that anger is a feeling everyone experiences sometimes and it is natural to feel angry. However, it is important to manage our anger so we do not hurt others.

2. Ask for volunteers to share their own experiences of times they felt angry. Ask children the following questions to introduce them to recognizing how they handle their anger:

   When you are angry, how does your body feel? *Responses:* "My hands get sweaty."
   "My tummy feels upset." "My body feels like exploding." "My face feels hot and gets all red."

   How do you act when you're angry? *Responses:* "I shout terrible things at the other person." "I get very quiet." "I hit the person I'm angry with." "I run away."

   If you hit others or shout at them when you feel angry, how does the other person feel? And how do you feel afterwards? *Responses:* "They cry when I hit them. I feel sad." "They don't like it when I shout. Then I feel sorry I lost my temper."

   Who is in charge of your anger? *Response:* "I blame the person I'm angry at but *I* really am in charge of it." Some students will respond they are forced to hit or shout by the person they are angry with. This will open up a discussion about *who is in charge of how they handle their anger.* The class discussion is to enable them to realize that the same person is always in charge of the way they handle anger: themselves.

3. Because some of your students react to their angry feelings the way they have been taught in their homes, it is important to make them aware there are alternative ways of handling anger than those they have learned. For example, children who have seen angry feelings resulting in physical violence to themselves or other family members will not be aware there are other ways of dealing with anger. Point out to students that physical violence is not an acceptable way of handling their angry feelings. Explain that the purpose of this lesson is to become aware of how they handle their feelings when they become angry. Children then realize it is up to them to handle their anger in a way that does not hurt anybody.

4. Pass "I'm a Hit" activity sheets to your class. Together read the possible answers of the best ways to handle angry feelings. Ask students which answers suggest positive ways

for everyone in the conflict to feel good about the way the anger was handled and to circle the letters. Tell students to write the best ways to handle anger on the lines inside the baseball. Decide whether to complete the activity together or individually.

5. The correct answers are: A—I will calm down; C—I won't hit or shout; D—I will listen to the other person. Discuss why these answers are the best ways to handle angry feelings.

6. Discuss the following answers that are *not* the way to handle anger because they end up with someone being hurt: B—I will shout at the other person; E—I will hit the person I'm mad at.

Bulletin Board Link:

Baseballs are displayed with the caption "We're Hits Handling Our Anger!" An alternative activity is for students to write inside their baseballs their positive qualities. Their photos or pictures of themselves could be drawn inside the baseballs. The caption is "I'm a Hit on My Class List!"

I'M A HIT!

Do you want anybody to get hurt when you feel angry? Probably not! In the baseball, tell what you will do the next time you are angry so you will be a hit with others. Circle the letters below that tell you how to handle your anger.

A. I will calm down.

B. I will shout at the other person.

C. I won't hit or shout.

D. I will listen to the other person.

E. I will hit the person I'm mad at.

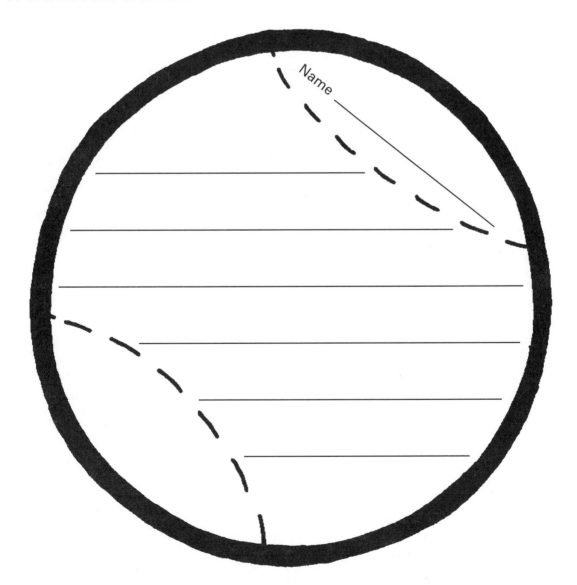

3–17. SMOOTH SOLUTIONS

Objective:

Students take a look at how they behave when they are angry and then analyze if that behavior is desirable or undesirable. Looking for a smooth solution the next time they feel "shook up" is the intended outcome.

Materials Needed:

- "Smooth Solutions" activity sheet
- Colored pencils or crayons

Directions:

1. Review with your class the fact that anger is a natural feeling we all experience. It is the *way* we handle our anger that results in appropriate or inappropriate behavior. Introduce the activity sheet by telling students they will be looking for smooth solutions when they feel shook up!

2. After students have received their "milkshakes," ask for volunteers who would like to share any experiences in which they felt shook up. Ask volunteers, "What was your behavior at the time?" and "How did you feel about your behavior afterward?" Provide students with an example of a situation in which a big sister gets "all shook up." The "Losin' It" scenario may be read to the class and then role-played in two ways:

   a. The big sister loses her temper and speaks in an angry voice to her little brother.

   b. The big sister calmly explains to her little brother the way she feels when he breaks her things.

Losin' It!

Big Sister: "I really lost it with my little seven-year-old brother when he unraveled my cassette tape. I yelled at him and he cried. Then when I cooled off later, I felt guilty."

Ask the students, "How could the anger have been handled differently? Should she repeat the same behavior? If not, how should she change it next time?" *Responses:* "Next time she will remember how guilty she felt when the yelling made her little brother cry. She will try not to get so shook up and instead explain to him how she feels when he breaks her things." "Maybe she could also remember to put her tapes away so her little brother can't reach them."

3. Direct the students' attention to their milkshake activity sheets. Ask them to recall a time when they felt all shook up and how they handled their anger at the time. Ask what were their feelings about their behavior and its effect on the person with whom they were angry. Finally, tell the class to write about what aspect of their behavior they will change in future situations. Assure them that this is going to be a learning process for the whole class. Nobody should feel embarrassed by the way they handled their anger as long as they realize *now* that there are alternative ways of handling their behavior when they are angry.

SMOOTH SOLUTIONS

If you find yourself in a conflict with someone, don't get all shook up! Choose a solution so that both of you feel like winners. Practice being able to look at your feelings when you are frustrated or angry by filling in the milkshake below with a SMOOTH SOLUTION.

Name: _____

When I am angry, I act

_____.

Right away or maybe later

I feel _____.

Here is what I am going

to change next time I

feel angry _____

_____

_____

_____

_____

3–18. CHILL!

Objective:

Children learn to walk away to avoid a confrontation if a physical threat is present or tempers are too volatile in a conflict that is "too hot to handle."

Materials Needed:

- "Chill!" activity sheet
- Pens; colored markers

Directions:

1. Ask your students when they think it is a good idea to avoid or to walk away from confronting a conflict. *Responses:* "If I think someone might hurt me, I will walk away." "If the person is swearing or yelling because they're so mad and can't calm down, I'll come back later to solve our problem."

2. Ask volunteers to give their experiences or role-play conflicts they have had that were "too hot to handle." Be sensitive to students who are reluctant to share personal experiences with the rest of the class. If you sense a child wants to share privately, invite him or her to have "chill-out" time between just the two of you.

3. Pass activity sheets for students to write about their own experiences handling conflicts when tempers (either their own or the other's) were out of control. They then write about how they would handle the conflict differently now.

Cooperative Group Activity:

Form small groups for a cooperative group activity. Ask *volunteers* in each group to role-play the activity they wrote about on their activity sheets. *Procedure:* **Act I.** Role-play activities from activity sheets. **Act II.** Children replay the conflict if they would choose to do it differently now.

CHILL!

Sometimes when you are in a conflict and somebody might get hurt, it's better to chill-out and walk away. You can solve it later after cooling down.

Write about how you handled it when a conflict was "too hot to handle." How did you cool it down?

_____

_____

_____

_____

_____

_____

_____

_____

3-19. MY TRIGGERS 'N TRAPS
3-20. MY TRIGGERS 'N TRAPS LOG

Objective:

Children recognize what sets off or triggers their anger, and the patterns or traps they get "stuck in" when their anger is triggered.

Materials Needed:

- "My Triggers 'n Traps" activity sheet
- "My Triggers 'n Traps Log" activity sheet
- Stapler or brown yarn to attach several copies per student for booklet

Directions:

1. Introduce this activity by having a class discussion about anger. You could begin by asking them to privately write things that often make them ANGRY! Say that we can call these things that make them angry over and over their *triggers.* Explain this information will not be shared unless they volunteer to share with the class. Allow time for children to think about and then to write down their triggers.

2. Ask for volunteers to share what triggers their anger. *Response:* "My little brother using my stuff always sets me off!" Be sure not to judge or comment upon their triggers; just listen. This part of the activity is valuable because as the volunteers share their triggers, other children will realize many of them share similar triggers.

3. After discussing their triggers, tell children to begin an awareness of the way they react to the anger that triggers them. Ask them to think about the patterns or traps of their behavior when they get triggered. Give them the example that if a child is triggered by her little brother taking her things and reacts repeatedly by hitting him, the repeated behavior of hitting is her "trap." Some people get trapped into quiet, withdrawn behavior when their anger is triggered. The idea is to try to find a *pattern* we revert to when we get angry. If children learn to tune in to their triggers and traps when they are young, they will be better able to control their anger as they get older and to channel it into constructive conflict resolution.

4. Pass the activity sheets to your class along with the "Triggers 'n Traps Log." Students complete their activity sheets first. Tell students that from their class discussion to now choose one of their triggers and to write it at the top of the page under "My Triggers." Under "My Traps" they are to write what they usually do or how they handle their anger when they feel mad. *Response:* "I punch when I get mad. I hit whoever made me mad." They then write *how they feel* after they have handled their anger by this behavior. *Response:* "I feel guilty because I usually make the person I'm mad at cry because I hurt them."

5. An important part of this activity is the last question, "Next time I get trapped I will . . ." This gives children the opportunity to alter any physical or emotional abuse they are inflicting on others and to plan alternative behavior.

6. Students use their "Triggers 'n Traps Log" to keep track of their anger for one week. They date the page daily for seven days. Each day they write and/or draw a picture (on the back of the sheet) about the trigger and then the trap. They describe how they behaved when they were triggered; for example: swearing, hitting, yelling, withdrawing, and pouting. They write how they think they handled their anger and then think about how they will handle it the next time it is triggered. They will begin to see a pattern of the traps emerge each time they get triggered after keeping a log for one week. You and the students will decide if these logs should be kept private or shared.

MY TRIGGERS 'N TRAPS

Have you ever thought about what makes you mad or what *triggers* your anger? Do the same things make you angry over and over again? If so, you may be caught in a *trap.*

Answer the questions below to find your triggers and traps. Keep a "Triggers 'n Traps Log" for several days so you can see how you handle the anger and avoid the traps that "trigger" you.

My Triggers

_____ usually makes me mad or triggers my anger. It happens over and over again.

Other times _____ triggers my anger.

My Traps

When my anger is triggered, usually I _____

_____

Afterward I usually feel _____

_____

When my anger is triggered other times, I _____

_____

Afterward I usually feel _____

_____

Next time I get triggered I will _____

_____

MY TRIGGERS 'N TRAPS LOG

Wow, did I get ANGRY today! Here's what happened:

Today I got triggered by: _____

_____

_____

_____

My trap was: _____

_____

_____

_____

Here's how I handled my anger: _____

_____

_____

_____

I feel _____ about the way I handled my anger.

Next time I'll: _____

_____

_____

_____

_____

3–21. WE'RE HOT STUFF! (AT COOLING DOWN)

Objective:

Children learn there are often patterns to their angry feelings, triggers, and traps. They learn the importance of cooling down when angry.

Materials Needed:

- "We're Hot Stuff! (At Cooling Down)" activity sheet
- Magazine and newspaper pictures of calm people and pictures of angry people
- "Hot" table with items such as hot spices, sunscreen, sunglasses, heating pad, etc.
- "Cool" table with items such as plastic ice cubes and tray, styrofoam cup coolers, etc.

Directions:

1. Ask for students to volunteer how they cool down when they feel angry. *Responses:* "I know if I lose it I'll do something I'll be sorry for later so I turn on my music." "I chill out by going to my room."

2. Have children privately recall a conflict in which they totally "lost it" and later regretted they did not cool down first. After being given a few moments, ask if a volunteer would like to share his or her story with the class. *Response:* "I lost my temper with my little brother and hit and swore at him. When he cried I felt sorry I hadn't waited until I didn't feel so angry."

3. Write the word "pattern" on the board. Ask students what the term means. *Response:* "A pattern is something that repeats itself over and over." Go over your classroom daily routine as an example of a pattern. Ask for some other examples of patterns. *Response:* "My everyday pattern is to watch a half hour of TV when I come in from playing after school, then I have dinner and then I have to do homework, have a bath and then read before going to sleep."

4. Pass activity sheets to your class to complete. Explain that before they can cool down, children first need to recognize their patterns of angry behavior they have had in the past as well as who or what triggered their anger.

5. After activity sheets are completed, inquire how many noticed a pattern to their behavior when angry and also a pattern as to whom or what usually triggered their anger. Ask for a volunteer to share his or her patterns of anger, triggers, and traps. *Response:* "I discovered I always yell at my mom when she tells me to clean up my room. That always sets me off because it's *my* room! Then I usually fall into the trap of refusing to clean it up and end up losing TV!" Ask your class if others have experienced the same or similar patterns of their own. *Responses:* Most hands will probably go up, making everyone realize that *we all have similar patterns when we are angry.* Ask who would like to tell how they would handle their behavior if they changed their patterns of anger and how they would feel about the changes.

Art Link:

Students cut hot chili peppers out of red paper and write on each pepper the best ways to cool down when angry. Each student could do several peppers, make holes in each, and tie green yarn inside the holes. Twine is passed to each student so they can hang their peppers from twine "branches." Hang the branches from your classroom ceiling.

WE'RE H ☀ T STUFF!

(AT COOLING DOWN)

How do you *cool down* when you're angry? If you don't stop to calm down, you may say or do something you'll be sorry for later. On the lines below become aware of what sets off your anger, how you usually handle it, and how you feel about it.

When I am angry I usually act _____

and afterwards I feel _____

How do I handle anger other times? _____

_____

How do I feel about this behavior? _____

What usually sets off my anger? _____

_____

Do the same things set off my anger over and over? _____

Here is what I will do to cool down next time I get angry: _____

_____

_____

_____

I want to feel _____ after our conflict is over.

I want the other person to feel _____

after our conflict is over.

3–22. FOLLOW THE YELLOW BRICK ROAD

Objective:

Primary children (can be adapted for older students) review the BBQ—Better Be Quiet—Recipe to calm down when they feel angry.

Materials Needed:

- "Follow the Yellow Brick Road" activity sheet
- Yellow markers or crayons (unless yellow paper is used)
- Pencils, pens, scissors

Directions:

1. Tell students you are going to make a yellow brick road in your classroom! (Explain the concept of the road from *The Wizard of Oz* to students who are unfamiliar with it.)

2. Pass activity sheets to the children. Read the top of the page together to give them directions. Ask three students to read the choices of answers to the question, "How are you going to handle your feelings next time you get mad?" Tell them to circle the letter of the correct answer. The correct answer is letter "M."

3. Ask for volunteers to tell why they think hitting (letter "A") and yelling (letter "B") when they are mad are not good ways to solve conflicts. *Responses:* "Hitting is not a good way to solve a conflict. And the other kid might hit you back and then you're into a fight!" "Yelling at the person you're mad at doesn't help solve the problem. If you calm down first you can try to work it out together."

4. Have a class discussion about what students can do to contribute to getting along together to create a more peaceful school. Write their responses on the board. Children write their own ideas on their bricks. *Response:* "Kids should not stand by and watch a bully bullying somebody."

Around-the-school-link:

Involve a few other classrooms or the whole school in creating a winding yellow brick road for the front hall. The caption is "At (name of school) We Follow the Yellow Brick Road to . . ." Sentence-stem completion choices are: Positive Self-Esteem; Good Ways to Solve Conflicts; Peacemaking; Our Behavior Code; Being Cooperative and Responsible Kids. The road could lead to a display in the gym or another room that extends the theme you choose. For example, display pictures drawn by the primary grades and plays or conflict-solving situations written (or a time for a performance for the school) by older students for the captions "Good Ways to Solve Conflicts" or "Peacemaking."

FOLLOW THE YELLOW BRICK ROAD

Make your own yellow brick road leading to good ways to solve conflicts at your school. Below circle the letter that tells how you are going to handle your feelings next time you get MAD. Then write your idea for a more peaceful school.

M—I will remember BBQ (Better Be Quiet) and calm down first.

A—I will hit the person I am mad at.

D—I will yell at the person to show how mad I am.

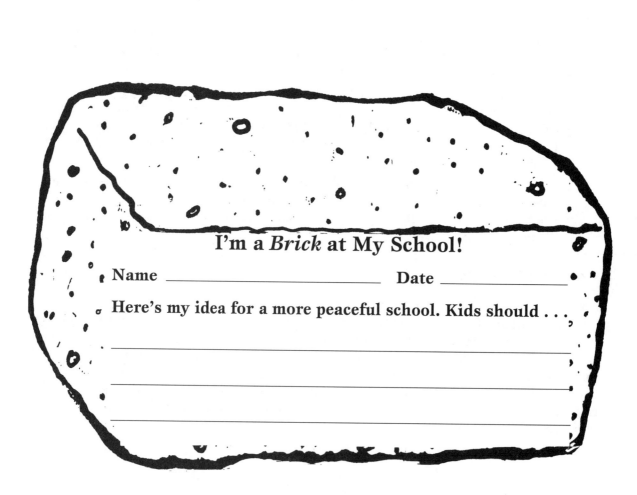

I'm a *Brick* at My School!

Name _____   Date _____

Here's my idea for a more peaceful school. Kids should . . .

_____

_____

_____

3–23. PUT A LID ON YOUR ANGER!
3–24. I-SCREAMERS
3–25. BUBBLE TROUBLE

Objective:

Children become aware that if they do not learn how to cool down when they have angry feelings, they may say or do something to hurt others.

Materials Needed:

- "Put a Lid on Your Anger!" "I-Screamers," and "Bubble Trouble" activity sheets
- Colored markers; crayons; scissors

Directions:

1. Have a class discussion about times children have been angry and said or done something hurtful to someone they were angry with or someone who happened to be present at the time they were angry. *Responses:* "I felt so sad after I made my little sister cry when I screamed at her when I was really mad at my best friend." "I hit someone I thought had taken my assignment and felt awful when I found out it was inside my book."

2. Pass the "Put a Lid on Your Anger!" activity sheets to students. Ask them to choose two good ideas for handling their angry feelings from the five possible choices. Remind them to put them in the correct order from the onset of their anger to what they would do next. The correct answers are:

    1. Be quiet and calm down. Plan what you will do.

    2. Tune in to *both* of your feelings.

3. Discuss why the other three ideas are not good choices when children feel angry. Ask the questions: Why is "Start to yell at the other person" not a good choice? *Response:* "Yelling does not lead to a resolution. It just makes the other person angrier." Why is "Hit the person you're angry with" not a good choice? *Response:* "Hitting won't solve a problem. You might hurt the other person and will also be in trouble." Why is "Call the other person names" not a good choice? *Response:* "If you want to let the other person know why you feel angry and then solve your problem, you have to talk it out. If you make others even madder by calling them names, they won't want to listen or to work it out with you."

4. As follow-up activities, distribute the "I-Screamers" and "Bubble Trouble" activity sheets. The concepts taught in "Put a Lid on Your Anger!" are reviewed while children enjoy doing an ice cream puzzle and also enjoy finding the lost message in Wilbert's bubbles. Shout at. Answers for "I-Screamers" puzzle: ***Down:*** 1. wait, 4. never; ***Across:*** 2. calm, 3. tune.

Bulletin Board Link for "Put a Lid on Your Anger!":

As an alternative to the activity on the activity sheet, pass out the sheets without the lines inside the paint can. Students write essays inside about times they have not handled their anger well and how they would handle the same problem now that they know the steps to cooling down when they are angry. They may begin their essays with "I can . . . ." The paint cans are colored and cut out. The caption is "We Paint Peaceful Solutions to Anger."

Bulletin Board Link for "I-Screamers":

Display a huge ice cream cone in the hall or on a wall of your classroom. Children cut the ice cream scoops from their activity sheets to write inside the scoops their own best alternatives to screaming or hitting when they feel angry. Ask them to each give his or her one best idea. Encourage children to then color their scoops in unusual flavors (have a contest for new flavors they make up) so that you have a colorful display. The caption is "Here's the Scoop on Cool Ways to Handle Anger!"

Bulletin Board Link for "Bubble Trouble":

Make a bubble border and a large bubble for each child in your class. Inside the bubbles, students write their own best ideas for handling their anger so they don't hurt anyone. The caption is "Bubblicious Ways to Handle Our Anger."

Name _____

PUT A LID ON YOUR ANGER!

Have you ever been very angry and said or done something that hurt somebody else? If so, have a plan for the next time you are angry. In the paint can below, write *what you will do when you start to feel angry.* Choose *two good ideas* from the list below. Be sure to put them in the correct order beginning with the first thing to do when you're angry.

Start to yell at the other person.

Tune in to *both* of your feelings.

Hit the person you're angry with.

Be quiet and calm down. Plan what you will do.

Call the other person names.

1. _____

_____

2. _____

_____

Name _____

I-SCREAMERS

Do you like to hear screaming? Not many people do!
Sometimes we forget that nobody likes to hear screaming. Do *you* sometimes scream?

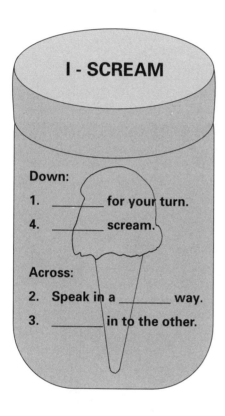

I - SCREAM

Down:

1. _____ for your turn.

4. _____ scream.

Across:

2. Speak in a _____ way.

3. _____ in to the other.

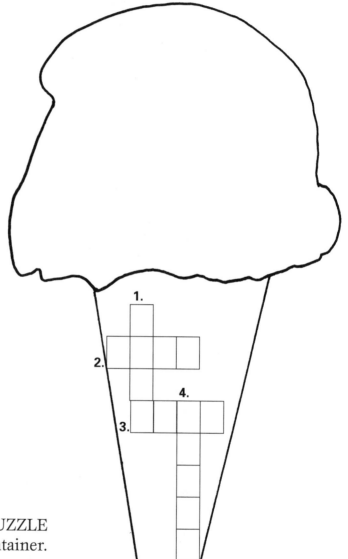

Fill in the I-SCREAM CONE PUZZLE words from the clues in the container. They will tell you how to handle angry feelings. Color your favorite flavor!

Choose your answers from the words below:

never   wait   tune   mad   calm   always   loud

BUBBLE TROUBLE

Part of Wilbert's message got lost in his bubbles. Figure out the lost words of his conflict message:

"Don't _____ _____ the other person when you feel angry."

3-26. THE ANGER ESCALATOR

Objective:

Students learn how their angry feelings can escalate.

Materials Needed:

- "The Anger Escalator" activity sheet
- Colored pencils
- Optional: plasticine

Directions:

1. Some of your students may not be familiar with an *escalator*. Ask for a volunteer to give a description of an escalator. *Response*: "An escalator is a moving stairway."

2. Write the term "escalate" on the board. Ask students for their meanings of the word. *Responses:* "Climb." "Grow." "Rise." "Step up."

3. Ask your class to remember the last time they felt very angry and to recall the stages of anger as their angry feelings *escalated* or grew. (Pause.) Solicit responses from students who volunteer to share their experiences of anger escalation.

4. Pass out activity sheets. Instruct students to choose a recent angry experience to recall and to write about it on the lines provided.

5. After completing their experiences, ask them to write descriptions in the four steps of the angry escalator about how they felt as their anger grew. Assure them that it is natural for people to have angry feelings that grow quickly and that it is important to be aware of each step. Explain that if we are aware of each step of our anger, we are better able to control our anger *before it controls us.*

6. When students have completed their anger escalators, ask for volunteers to copy their anger escalators on the board. This sharing enables students to realize that others have the same angry feelings as themselves. Children then become aware of the importance of recognizing the next stage of anger before it appears, thus being able to control the escalation before it is out of control.

Art and Hall Display Link:

A fun way to demonstrate we are the "captains" of our angry feelings is an activity building little planes of plasticine. The aim is to show, by comparing our anger to a plane, that we need to be "in control" from the moment it (the anger) takes off. Students enjoy making their own planes made of plasticine complete with windows and small faces of the passengers. The child who makes the plane is the captain. (Students could pair up and co-captain a plane, constructing it together.) The caption for each of the planes is "Captain _____ is in control upon take off!"

THE ANGER ESCALATOR

Think about a time you felt very angry. On the steps of the escalator *write your feelings* and *draw your face to show how you felt angrier and angrier*. Here are some examples you may want to use for your angry escalator.

Step 1. Starting to get angry, face getting red *or* getting hot *or* stomach hurting

Step 2. Anger is creeping up, screaming at the other *or* clenching fists

Step 3. Feeling very angry, hitting *or* throwing something

Step 4. Anger is out of control, boiling mad

3-27. SNOWBALLS

Objective:

Children learn to calm down when they feel angry so the anger does not get out of control.

Materials Needed:

- "Snowballs" activity sheet
- Pencils

Directions:

1. Discuss that a "snowball effect" means that something starts out small and then grows and grows. This is compared to a snowball that rolls in the snow and gets bigger and bigger. Give the following example: "You are angry with your sister for not rubbing hard enough to get out the dirty spot that she put on your best sweater. But you decide not to tell her you are angry with her. Another accident happens again when she borrows your jacket and gets another spot on it. You are now angrier about the dirt on the jacket because you're still mad about the sweater." Explain that this example is how the snowball effect works.

2. Pass out the "Snowballs" activity sheets to your students. Before you ask them to write about their own examples of "snowball effects" in their lives, have volunteers tell about how angry events they have had started out over something small and then grew into something big. After they describe the events, ask how they might have handled them differently if they had cooled down before their anger "snowballed" out of control. *Response:* "My mom told me to turn off the TV and do my homework. But I didn't have any homework that day. I had two tests and finished my math at school so I had no work to take home. I lost my temper with my mom because it was the second day in a row she made me turn off my favorite TV show. The day before I had already studied for my tests and I got really mad because mom didn't wait to hear my side. It snowballed. Next time, I'll calm down and I will explain my situation to her."

3. Ask students to complete on the activity sheets their own examples of an incident that had started out small and got bigger and bigger and then made them angry. Have students volunteer what they would do differently so that the conflict would not "snowball" again.

Bulletin Board Link:

Make a large snowball for each child out of white posterboard. Inside they write or draw a picture about a conflict they had that "snowballed" out of control. They write how they would cool down next time. Caption for the bulletin board is "Our Snowballs Don't Hurt Others." Decorate the display with puffs of cotton sprinkled with silver glitter and a snowman with your class picture inside.

Name _____

SNOWBALLS

Anger can start out about something small and get bigger and bigger like a snowball effect. Can you remember a time when you were angry about something small and it got bigger and bigger? Write about it below.

_____

_____

_____

_____

_____

_____

_____

_____

_____

Write about what you will do next time so it won't get bigger and bigger or "snowball."

_____

_____

_____

_____

_____

_____

_____

_____

3–28. WILBERT'S CRUMBY COOKIES

Objective:

Children learn they are responsible for controlling their anger; it does not control them.

Materials Needed:

- "Wilbert's Crumby Cookies" activity sheet
- Scissors; pencils
- *Optional:* light brown paper for cookies; various colors of paper for cookies if variety is desired; silver foil

Directions:

1. Tell students you are going to pass them cookie (activity) sheets that the character Wilbert has mixed up. If this is the first activity with the Wilbert character, explain that he often clumsily gets himself into predicaments. If you have done previous Wilbert activities, children will be familiar with him.

2. Pass out the activity sheets. Children will see from the illustration that Wilbert is upset because he dropped his cookies, and then the answer on the cookies got all mixed up. Ask students to figure out the answer on the spilled cookies to the following fill-in-the-blank: **When you're in a conflict, _____ doesn't control you; you control it.** *Answer:* Anger.

3. Give students time to figure out the answer in the message and then ask them to write it on the activity sheet space. Discuss the answer together. Ask them what happens sometimes when people allow anger to control them when they are in a conflict with someone else. *Responses:* "They yell at the other person." "They start punching out the person they're mad at." "They say really mean things."

4. Ask children what happens when people realize they are in control of their anger. *Responses:* "They cool off and don't hit the other person." "Instead of shouting or swearing, they try to work it out."

Cooperative-Group Activity and Bulletin Board Link:

Divide your class into small groups. Have students cut out circles from light brown paper for their cookies. Cookies may be all the same or a different set of cookies is made by each cooperative group. *Examples:* fruit-filled, chocolate (will need a white strip of paper pasted on for writing), animal shapes, etc. Each student puts his or her name on a cookie and passes it to the members of his or her group to sign one positive quality. Cookies are then filled with all the positive things the group wrote about the child whose name is on the cookie. Display these on the bulletin board's large "cookie sheets" made of long rectangles of silver foil. The caption is "Our Sweet Celebration."

Cookie Link:

If all this work on a cookie theme makes your students and yourself hungry, treat yourselves with some real (low-fat if there are dietary concerns in your class) cookies! Or enjoy fortune cookies for a special treat for your class.

WILBERT'S CRUMBY COOKIES

Wilbert tried to stuff too many cookies into his cookie bag and some of them fell out! He had an answer to a question on the cookies and now it's all mixed up! Help Wilbert put his cookie answer back together to solve this sentence's missing word.

The question is: this doesn't control you; **you** control it.

The answer is: _____ .

Make up a funny story about something Wilbert does that causes a conflict. Write it in the cookie bag.

Title: _____

_____

_____

_____

_____

_____

_____

_____

3–29. TASTY TOPPINGS

Objective:

Children learn sayings to use when they want to calm the other person down and create a conciliatory mood to solve the conflict.

Materials Needed:

- "Tasty Toppings" activity sheet
- Scissors; paste; colored markers

Directions:

1. Ask if anyone in your class said something when he or she was angry and was sorry about it later. *Response:* "I swore at a friend when I got mad. Then I was sorry about it when she said she couldn't come over to my house anymore."

2. Explain to students that the activity sheet they will receive will give them some "tasty toppings" or sayings to have ready to use when they get into a conflict. Tell them that these sayings will make the other person in the conflict more agreeable to solving it so both will feel happy with the solution.

3. Pass activity sheets to your class. Explain that they are to cut out only the strawberries that contain the letters of the sayings *they agree* would be good to use when conflict solving. They then paste the strawberries on the shortcake. If students choose the correct "tasty toppings," the letters will form the word that is to be written at the bottom of the page. The Tasty Bonus Word is *yummy*.

4. After students have completed their cutting and pasting and written the tasty bonus word at the bottom of the page, discuss the sayings that do not work well to solve conflicts. These sayings are letters **D, A, P,** and **O**. Ask how they would feel if approached by someone with any of these sayings when trying to solve a conflict. *Response:* "I would get even angrier and would not be in a conflict-solving mood!"

Bulletin Board Link:

Display a huge sundae and a large red cherry (or other sundae topping) for each student to write his or her favorite "tasty topping" to have ready to use in a conflict. The caption is "Our Tastiest Toppings," "Pick Your 'Berry' Best Conflict Topping," or "A Taste of What to Say to Solve Conflicts." Or students' cherries are all displayed in a large bowl (made of cellophane or drawer liner paper cut into the shape of a bowl) with the caption "Conflict Solving Is a Bowl of Cherries for Us."

TASTY TOPPINGS

When you feel angry, do you say things you are sorry about later? Instead of saying mean things to others when you're mad, have some "tasty toppings" ready to say. Cut out only the strawberries with the letters of the sayings you will use in a conflict and paste on the strawberry sundae.

Tasty Bonus Word: Write at the bottom of the next page the word formed by the letters of the toppings you chose. *Clue:* It's how the strawberry sundae looks.

D—It's all your fault, you loser!

M—I think we can work this problem out together.

A—My way is the only way to work this out.

P—I'm going to get even with you for this!

Y—I'm ready to listen to your side of the story! Then I need you to listen to mine.

M—Let's do TLC (Tune in, Listen, and Choose the best solution) together

O—I'll make you sorry for doing this.

Y—Hey, let's get together later to work this out. I think we need to cool off more first.

U—Before we start to solve this together, let's try the BBQ Recipe (Better Be Quiet!).

TASTY TOPPINGS

Tasty Bonus Word is: ___ ___ ___ ___ ___

3–30. DON'T GET TICKED!

Objective:

Students review concepts of anger they learned in previous activity lessons while playing a game of tic-tac-toe.

Materials Needed:

- "Don't Get Ticked!" activity sheet
- Pencils, pens or colored markers
- Large tic-tac-toe grid numbered one to nine inside each square on the board

Directions:

1. Ask your students to raise their hands if they have played the game of tic-tac-toe. After seeing how many are familiar with the game, ask for a student to explain the object of the game. *Response:* "To win the game, you must complete a straight or diagonal row or column of three X's or O's in winning rows." Display an example on a large tic-tac-toe grid on the board.

2. Pass out activity sheets to students as you announce that they will now be playing a game of tic-tac-toe as they answer questions reviewing what they have learned about handling their anger.

3. Call on a student to read the activity instructions at the top of the page. Write X = YES and O = NO on the board to remind them as they fill in their tic-tac-toe grids.

4. Instruct children to answer the questions on their activity sheets by writing an "X" or an "O" in the corresponding number inside the tic-tac-toe grids. Tell them that although this game is usually played between two people, they are going to play it individually for this activity. Ask them not to share with others the numbers of their winning squares before you discuss each question and answer together as a class. As each question is discussed and the answer for it is given, have the student who gives the answer write it on your grid on the board. *The correct answers are as follows:* The winning numbers are in the column 2, 5, and 8. They are all YES answers.

```
O | X | O
---------
O | X | X
---------
X | X | O
```

DON'T GET TICKED!

How do you handle your angry feelings? Answer the following questions in the numbered boxes in the tic-tac-toe game. Answer with an "X" for YES and "O" for NO. If you complete a straight or diagonal row or column of three X's or three O's, you WIN the game!

1.	2.	3.
4.	**5.**	**6.**
7.	**8.**	**9.**

1. Hitting the person you're angry with is the best way to solve the problem for both of you.
2. When you feel really angry, cool down before starting to solve the conflict.
3. The best way to solve a conflict is to shout or swear at the person you are angry with.
4. Look out only for your own interests when you are angry with someone.
5. Make sure you're feeling angry about what's happening NOW and not about something in the past.
6. Use the TLC (Tender Loving Care) approach when you are feeling angry with somebody.
7. People are going to have *differences* and if they turn into conflicts they *can* be handled so everybody is happy with the solution.
8. Feeling angry is OK; hurting others physically or emotionally when you're angry is *not* OK.
9. It's not important to listen to the other person when you're angry.

3–31. JUST PICTURE IT!

Objective:

Children learn the steps of brainstorming as part of the problem-solving process when confronting a conflict.

Materials Needed:

- "Just Picture It!" activity sheet
- Brainstorming steps visually displayed

Directions:

1. Write "brainstorm" on the board along with the responses students give you when you ask them for their ideas of the meaning of the term "brainstorm." *Responses:* "To give out lots of ideas to solve a problem." "To say whatever solutions you think of and then choose the one that makes the most sense." "Just say a bunch of ways to find an answer, then pick the best one of all of them." After you have listened to several responses, congratulate your students on having just completed a brainstorming session!

2. Have the following brainstorming points on display in your classroom or written on the board:

> **Step 1. Say in one sentence what the problem is.**
>
> **Step 2. Say what you want to happen to solve the problem.**
>
> **Step 3. Think of lots of possibilities to get what you want.**
>
> **Step 4. Choose the very best of all your possible solutions.**
>
> **Step 5. Put your solution to work and decide if it was the best after all!**

3. Take your students through the above steps of brainstorming, and have a brainstorming session about an everyday problem in your classroom. Make the point with your class that when they are giving their ideas for brainstorming, all ideas are listened—even if some seem crazy—and nobody puts anybody down when suggestions are made. Explain that they are creating a pool of responses so they can have lots of possibilities for a solution; then they will choose the best one.

    Example: Give the following problem to your class to brainstorm. "Here is the classroom problem: Kids are pushing ahead of others already in line. Give me some possible solutions." You then write their brainstorming solutions on the board:

    "Tell the teacher."

    "Let the kid into the line to save trouble."

    "Yell at the person who shoved."

"All the kids who were pushed should tell the pushy person to go to the back of the line."

"Shove the person out of the way."

Discuss not only the best of these possible solutions but also why the other possibilities were not chosen as the best solution. Students will probably arrive at solution #4. If they do not, spend some time discussing why it is the best solution to the problem.

4. Pass activity sheets to your students. These sheets are to be completed individually as each student gives one problem that he or she would like to solve by going through the brainstorming steps. They write them in the "thought cloud bubble" at the top of the ladder. After the sheets are completed, students share in small groups their possible solutions and then the one they chose as the best solution.

Name _____

JUST PICTURE IT!

When you have a problem, do you think of different ways to solve it? If you do, then you can choose the very best solution. We call this *brainstorming!* Follow the steps to brainstorming on the ladder below, picture several ways to solve it, and write them in the thought bubble. Choose the *best* solution for your problem and mark it by putting a *happy face* in front of the number.

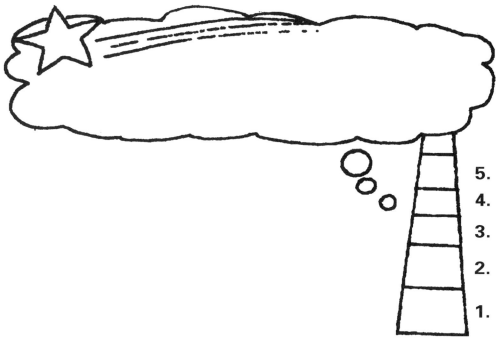

Step 1. Say in one sentence what the problem is.

Step 2. Say what you want to happen to solve the problem.

Step 3. Think of lots of possibilities to get what you want.

Step 4. Choose the very best of all your possible solutions.

Step 5. Put your solution to work and decide if it was the best after all!

My problem is _____

I want this to happen _____

_____

Possible solutions are _____

_____

_____

The very best solution I choose is _____

_____

3–32. POTATTLE CHIPS

Objective:

Children learn to solve their own problems instead of repeatedly "tattling" on others.

Materials Needed:

- "Potattle Chips" activity sheet
- Colored markers, crayons

Directions:

1. Have a class discussion about children who repeatedly tell on other children. Before you begin this talk, make it clear that any incidents involving bullying, physical violence, weapons, drugs, or anything else involving the safety of others should immediately be reported to an adult. This is not tattling but following the rules of safety.

2. Define a "tattler" or a "tattle-taler" as one who tells on others repeatedly for very small incidents other than those involving safety issues. Tell them a good way to tell if a person is a tattle-taler is if they repeatedly seek adult help for incidents they could have worked out themselves *if* they had used their problem-solving skills. Ask how many like to be with tattletalers. Not many will say they like to be around them. *Responses:* "Kids who tell on others all the time are really annoying." "Sometimes they just want to get attention for themselves."

3. Tell your class you are going to pass them an activity sheet with potattle chips. Explain they are called "potattle chips" for this lesson because the children are going to chip away at others who tattle repeatedly. They will help the tattle-taler by teaching him or her some problem-solving skills to use instead of telling on someone. Pass out the sheets.

4. Together read the directions and the selections to choose for problem-solving at the top of the sheet. Depending on the ages of your students, complete together or individually the problem-solving skills they would choose to use instead of tattling. They are to then write the letters that correspond to those skills in the potattle chips. Discuss the skills they would *not* choose (**D** and **F**) and why those actions would *not* help to solve the problem but may make the other person angrier.

Bulletin Board Link:

The potattle chip idea could also be used for an anti-bullying display. Students make a huge chip container and one large chip for each student. Children fill in their potato chips with their best ideas to discourage bullying in your school. Hang their chips above the container with the caption "Our Class Chips Away at Bullying."

Cooperative-Group Link:

Children form groups of five or six. One large chip container is made for each group. (A group of students could make these containers and one large potato chip made of yellow construction paper or posterboard for each student.) Inside each chip they write the best idea they have to discourage bullying in the classroom or school. Each group's containers and chips are displayed together with the caption "Cooperation Chips Away at Bullying" or "Cooperation Chips Away at Violence."

POTATTLE CHIPS

Do you know someone who always tells on others for every little thing? Instead of "tattle-taling," what could "tattle-talers" do? Write the letters of things they could do to solve their own problems in the *potattle chips* below. **Remember:** Telling on someone who bullies others is not tattle-taling; it is safety!

A. Ask why the other is angry.
B. Say to the angry person, "Hey, let's work this out together."
C. If you did something to make the other angry, say "I'm sorry."
D. Yell back louder than the other yelled.
E. Say, "When you yell at me, I feel angry because I don't like yelling."
F. Hit the person who makes you angry.
G. Say, "I'm ready to listen to why you're so mad."
H. "I will not put up with your bullying. If it happens again, I will get help."

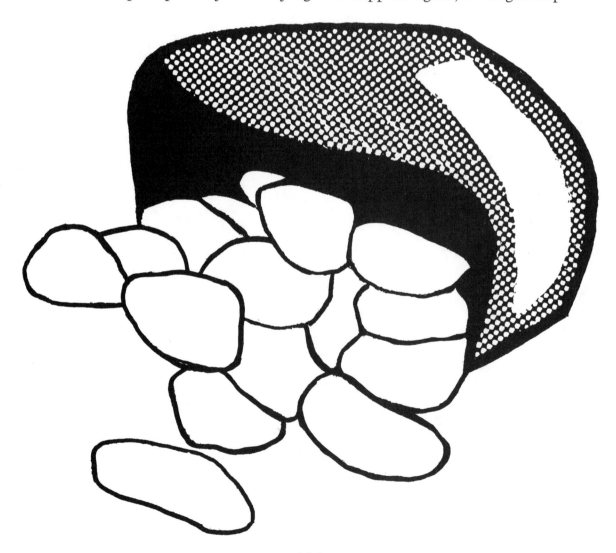

3–33. GOOD STUFF!

Objective:

Students learn creative problem-solving by finding creative solutions to everyday problem situations they can relate to.

Materials Needed:

- "Good Stuff!" activity sheet
- Space for a Creative Problem-Solving Center; box for creative problems and solutions; books on lateral thinking puzzles (suggestions for the classroom: *Lateral Thinking Puzzles* by Paul Sloane and *Challenging Lateral Thinking Puzzles* by Paul Sloane and Des McHale)

Directions:

1. If you have not already introduced your class to creative problem-solving then get ready for a special time! It is said that the human mind once stretched will not go back to its original dimensions. If you teach your students to think *laterally* or *creatively*, they will never go back to the "old way" of looking at solutions for problems without any creativity. You may want to make time each week for doing lateral-thinking puzzles with your class. For example, every Friday students could gather for "Creative Puzzle Time" with problems taken from creative problem-solving or lateral puzzles books. Children also enjoy taking turns thinking of their own puzzles that elicit challenging solutions from their classmates. You will find that all of you will look forward to this creative session, which brightens up a Friday!

2. Write the term "creative" on the board and ask students what the word means to them. *Response:* "A new way of looking at something." Write the term "creative problem-solving" on the board and ask for a definition. *Response:* "Finding a new way when you're trying to solve a problem."

3. Pass activity sheets to students. Tell them this will give them the chance to solve some problems that may remind them of their own problems. If you divide your class into small groups, they can brainstorm solutions for the problems. Or students could problem-solve in pairs or individually. Remember to stress that a solution is correct if it works; there is no single solution for lateral or creative puzzles. It is important to remind groups not to discourage a child in the group who is thinking creatively for the first time by dismissing his or her answer by saying, "That's a stupid idea!" or "That would never work." Instead, the child who is trying—but not yet finding solutions that work—could be encouraged by classmates saying, "Try again. You were close this time!" or "That's good stuff! Let's think of even more ideas to solve it."

4. Some possible solutions follow; however, students will think of many more and varied solutions. There are "textbook answers" for creative problems, but don't let them get in the way of creatively thinking of solutions to the problem. If the solution works, then that solution is "right" although it is not a "textbook answer." *Some suggested solutions follow:*

Suggested Solution for #1: You could put a barrier (chairs, a toddler folding gate, etc.) to block the stairs so Bud can't go upstairs while the family is sleeping.

Suggested Solution for #2: The old garbage can could be placed upside down next to other full garbage cans put out on the day garbage is collected or the old garbage can could be thrown into a dumpster if one is accessible.

Suggested Solution for #3: You could take your mom's other high-heeled shoe to the butcher (remember it's a large supermarket, so a butcher is probably there) and ask him or her to cut off the other heel! Also, you could ask him to even out both heels. Now your mom can wear both shoes with no heels to the party and you won't be late!

5. Encourage students to think of their own problems for classmates to solve. They can start by writing them on the back of the activity sheet that may turn into their own "Good Stuff" books as they get the creative juices going. Give them a date and time to give their problems to the whole class to solve creatively. Or if you have an ongoing Creative Problem-Solving Center, children will also enjoy problems you make up for them to solve. Think of a problem you've had or are presently faced with in your own life and ask for their creative solutions. If you and your class do these puzzles regularly throughout the school year, think of how your minds will stretch to being advanced lateral problem-solvers!

6. Keep all the problems and the children's creative solutions at your Creative Problem-Solving Center. Put together a **class book** of all your students' own puzzles, together think of a great creative title, and—at the end of the school year—bind it together with your class's year for your new students to use the following school year.

Creative Problem-Solving Center:

Cut off the bottom of the activity sheet and have lots of copies ready in your "We're Creative Problem-Solvers!" or "We're Lateral Thinkers!" center in your classroom. Students can write problems for their classmates to solve in creative ways and then place the sheet in a "creative thinking box" decorated by students with a light bulb and question marks. Also available at the center are lateral-thinking puzzle books that are changed each month. The books may gradually become more challenging as students become better acquainted with creative problem-solving. Also challenging quotations that inspire children are changed every month or so. A few suggestions for sayings to have on display in the center are:

"I think and think for months, for years; ninety-nine times and the conclusion is false. But the hundredth time I'm right." "Imagination is more important than knowledge."
—ALBERT EINSTEIN

"Success comes to those who realize it isn't coming to them and who go out to get it."
—ANONYMOUS

"The uncreative mind can spot wrong answers but it takes a very creative mind to spot wrong questions." —ANTONY JAY

"Man's mind stretched to a new idea never goes back to it original dimension."
—OLIVER WENDELL HOLMES

GOOD STUFF!

Thinking in a new way to find a solution to a problem is called **creative problem-solving**. Solve the problems below creatively. If your solution works, you solved the problem. That's *good stuff!*

Problem #1: Your parents are going to bed early. They tell you to put your dog, Bud, in the basement before you come to bed. When you try to get Bud to go to the basement, he won't go and he pretends to be sleeping! Nothing you can do will budge him. Bud is never allowed to go upstairs. If he does go upstairs during the night, you'll be in big trouble! You can't stay up all night to watch Bud, so what is a creative solution?

My creative solution is to _____

_____

_____

Problem #2: You are told to keep trying to get rid of an old garbage can at your house. You ask your dad how he expects you to get the garbage collectors to take the garbage can away. You tell him you tried before and left a HUGE note on the garbage can asking the collectors to "please take it away" and they still didn't take it away! Your dad says, "Be creative and figure it out!"

My creative solution is to _____

_____

_____

Problem #3: You and your mom are running late on your way to a family surprise birthday party. You stop to buy a cake for the party at the large supermarket on the other side of town. Suddenly your mom is really annoyed that her heel from one of her high-heeled shoes just broke off. She doesn't have time to go home to get new shoes! She asks what you think she can do.

My creative solution is to _____

_____

_____

On the back of this sheet, make up your own problem situation for your classmates to solve creatively. Give your own creative solution only *after* they have given you their creative ideas. Remember, their solutions are right if they work! There may be several creative solutions.

3-34. PUT YOURSELF IN SOMEBODY ELSE'S SHOES

Objective:

Children will learn the life skill of seeing a problem from another person's point of view.

Materials Needed:

- "Put Yourself in Somebody Else's Shoes" activity sheet
- Pictures cut from magazines, catalogs and newspapers to use as "gifts"

Directions:

1. Ask students to think about a recent conflict they had with someone. Have them recall how they felt at the time and also how they think the other person was feeling. Ask for volunteers to share their experiences. If you notice that children only relate their own feelings, remind them that the other part of this exercise is *to tell how they think the other person was feeling* at the time.

2. Pass activity sheets to your students. Ask them to tell about a recent conflict they have had but to tell the story by putting themselves in the other person's shoes. Inside the activity sheet shoe, tell them to *write about what the other person needed and was interested in.*

3. After students have completed their activity shoes, ask for volunteers to share their stories.

4. Announce to your class that they are going to play the game, "Put Yourself in Somebody Else's Shoes" (or you may call the game "Convince Me!"). Say that the object of the game is to convince your partner to give up your "gift." (A suggestion list for you to collect for a bag of "gifts" from which students choose are magazine pictures of a current kids' favorite tape or CD, an issue of a popular youth magazine, a sports T-shirt, a baseball cap, and other items children are interested in.)

5. Divide students into pairs. Each partner takes a turn convincing the other to give up the "gift" to him or her. No offer of physical force or money may be used. After about two minutes, ask students to change partners so that they will have the chance to put themselves in the other person's shoes! (The same "gift" is used.) They can see how it felt for their partners to hold on to their "gifts" while being convinced to give them up. They go through the same routine trying to convince the other to give up the "gift."

Note: Doing this activity with educators at a faculty meeting or conflict-solving workshop is lots of fun while, at the same time, enabling educators to put themselves in another's place. Collect a bag of items you feel would be fun and interesting, allowing one item for two people. Divide the group into partners, play the game together, and enjoy your colleagues' creativity.

PUT YOURSELF IN SOMEBODY ELSE'S SHOES

When you have a disagreement with others, do you try to see the problem from their viewpoints or just your own? In the shoe below, put yourself in the shoes of someone you have had (or are having) a conflict with by telling the problem as *they* see it, not as *you* see it. Explain what their needs and interests are in solving the conflict. When you get together with the person, you will see the problem from his or her point of view for a change!

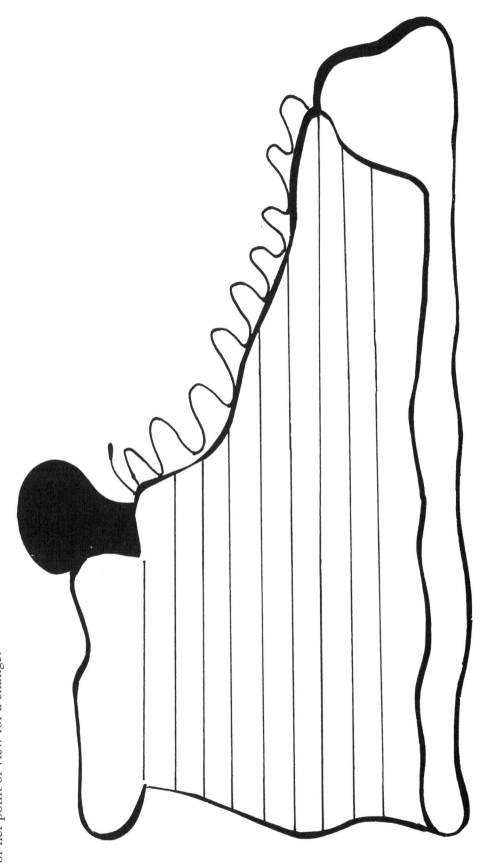

3-35. SPAGHETTI! SPAGHETTI!

Objective:

Children learn that often others are not going to share their opinions. Understanding and respecting others' opinions that are not the same as their own are intended outcomes.

Materials Needed:

- "Spaghetti! Spaghetti!" activity sheet
- *optional:* samples of various dry pasta

Directions:

1. Pass out the "Spaghetti! Spaghetti!" activity sheets. In addition to spaghetti, decide on two other pasta choices you will use when voting to determine your students' favorites. Macaroni/cheese and lasagne are probably the most popular. Tally on the board the favorite votes for each different pasta you survey. Ask students to tell you their favorite pasta dishes out of three choices you are going to give them. They are to vote for only one. First, ask how many of them think *everybody* will choose spaghetti as their favorite. Responses will probably show most of them will expect spaghetti to be the only choice from the class. Then ask who would choose spaghetti as their favorite pasta. Responses will probably show a large number who favor spaghetti. Write "spaghetti" on the board with the number of favorites next to it.

2. Not all students will be familiar with pasta other than spaghetti. If you or your students bring in samples of different dry pastas, display them and give students the opportunity to see the various choices of pasta that may include macaroni, lasagne, fettucini, manicotti, and rotini. Write your two other choices of pasta to tally on the board. Ask for a show of hands of favorites for each of the two and tally them on the board next to the spaghetti tally.

3. Ask students who did not choose to vote for any of the three pastas if they have choices other than those you offered and write them on the board. Or some may say they do not like to eat any pasta. Others may say they have never tried pasta. Discuss these differences together, stressing the importance of not imposing our tastes on other people and not judging them for their own differences and opinions.

4. After completing on the board their tallies on all the pastas, ask your class to view the differences and to copy the tallies on their sheets. Ask if those who chose spaghetti for their favorite and thought everyone else in the class would also choose spaghetti are surprised there are other choices. Responses will vary, but many will say they are surprised there are other favorites than spaghetti.

5. You may choose to complete the activity sheets together or individually. Make the connection to your students with the pasta tally on the board that not everybody shares the same opinions as they do. When they begin to realize there are many differences in opinions, they will then be able to look at a problem from somebody else's viewpoint.

6. Discuss differences in opinions about things other than food. For example, preferences for music, sports, and television programs differ from one person to the next. After discussion, students are to think of two more examples of areas of differences and write them on their activity sheets.

SPAGHETTI! SPAGHETTI!

Everybody loves spaghetti! Right? Take a vote and find out!

How many kids in your class choose spaghetti as their favorite pasta? _____

Name two other pastas and the number of kids' favorites for each one:

1. Pasta: _____   _____

2. Pasta: _____   _____

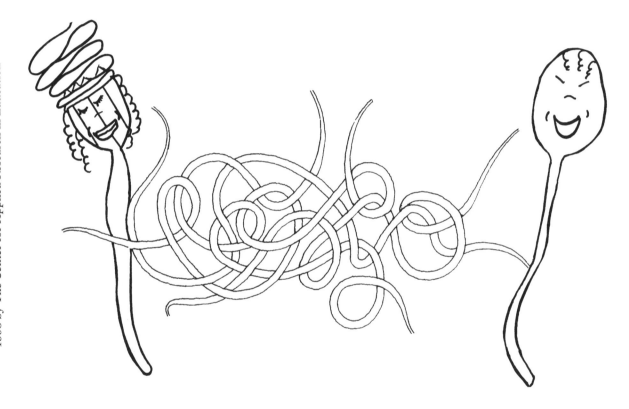

Do people have different opinions about other things also? Give two examples:

1. _____

   _____

2. _____

   _____

3–36. MY MAGIC GLASSES
3–37. HERE ARE MY MAGIC GLASSES
3–38. THE SAD HEART
3–39. MY HEART PATTERN

Objective:

Primary children learn what a problem looks like from somebody else's eyes with their *magic glasses.*

Materials Needed:

- "My Magic Glasses" and "The Sad Heart" activity sheets
- Here Are My Magic Glasses and My Heart patterns
- Glitter; glue; crayons; markers; stickers; stars; scissors
- Sturdy paper to trace the magic glasses; clear tape
- *optional for Heart Link:* red, pink, or white felt

Directions:

1. Announce to your children they are going to receive a pair of glasses they can put on when they want to look at a problem or conflict through somebody else's eyes. They can call them their "magic glasses." Pass the "My Magic Glasses" activity sheet to your class and the "Here Are My Magic Glasses" patterns for students to cut out and tape to a stick to use when they want to look at a problem through somebody else's eyes. The glasses are traced onto posterboard, cut out, and glued together. They are then decorated creatively by each child with glitter, stars, or stickers.

2. Discuss with children how they feel when someone's feelings get hurt. *Responses:* "I feel sad." "I feel sorry for them." Some children may not have learned to feel empathy for another person, so this may be their introduction to feeling sorry for someone who is hurt. This is a very important lesson for children to learn while they are young.

3. Read the story "The Sad Heart," together. Discuss the conflict through Terry's eyes. Then discuss what the problem looks like through Tod's eyes. Ask for volunteers to share similar experiences with the class.

4. Decide if your class will answer the question, "What could Terry say to Tod?" on their activity sheets individually (or if you will answer orally as a class with answers written on the board together).

5. When children have a conflict in your classroom, tell them it is "magic glasses" time. Ask each involved in the conflict to put on his or her magic glasses to take turns looking at the problem through the other child's eyes.

6. Pass "The Sad Heart" activity sheet to your class. Students dictate, draw, or write a story entitled "My Sad Heart Story," about a time they or someone they knew felt sad.

Heart Link:

Ask some of your students to cut out hearts, tracing from "My Heart" activity sheets. Use red felt for each child in your class for the hearts. They then cut out small squares of pink or white felt that they glue to the center of the heart to act as pockets to put things into. Children put their names on the front of each heart, at the bottom. The hearts are displayed in a place in your classroom that is easy for the children to reach. You may use these hearts in several ways. Here are a few suggestions:

- Use the heart pocket to keep track of the negative and positive feelings children have in the course of a day (or for older children over two or three days) as children put small plus or minus signs into their heart pockets each time they talk positively (plus sign) or negatively (minus sign) to themselves during the school day.

- Form cooperative groups and give each child a small heart or slip of paper for each child to give something positive they noticed about each of the other children in the group. (Any time you do an exercise with children giving positive comments to each other, monitor all groups to make sure nobody passes on a certain child or gives a put-down to a child in the group.)

- Use the heart pockets *for you to put little heart notes* as surprises for children from time to time. Use them to encourage a child about progress being made in behavior or in a certain subject, to a student new to the school, or for a child who is going through a difficult period at home (without mentioning the negative incident he or she is going through).

- Put your own heart on display with the children's hearts. They will enjoy putting their little hearts or slips of paper *in your heart pocket,* complimenting something you have done or encouraging *you.*

MY MAGIC GLASSES

When somebody's feelings are hurt, how do you feel? _____

_____

Do you try to see what the problem looks like from their eyes? _____

Cut out the magic glasses and tape them to a stick. Wear them when you want to see what the problem looks like in the other person's eyes. Read the story below.

The Sad Heart

Terry hits her little brother, Tod. He had ripped a page in her favorite book. He starts to cry and tells Terry she is mean! Terry wonders how Tod could say that when he tore up her book! If Terry puts on her magic glasses, she will see the problem from Tod's eyes. He would say, "I was looking at Terry's favorite book and being careful. When I stood up, I stepped on the page and it ripped. But it was an accident. I feel awful. I love 'dat' book!" Tod starts to cry.

What could Terry say to Tod?

_____

_____

_____

_____

_____

© 1998 by The Center for Applied Research in Education

HERE ARE MY MAGIC GLASSES

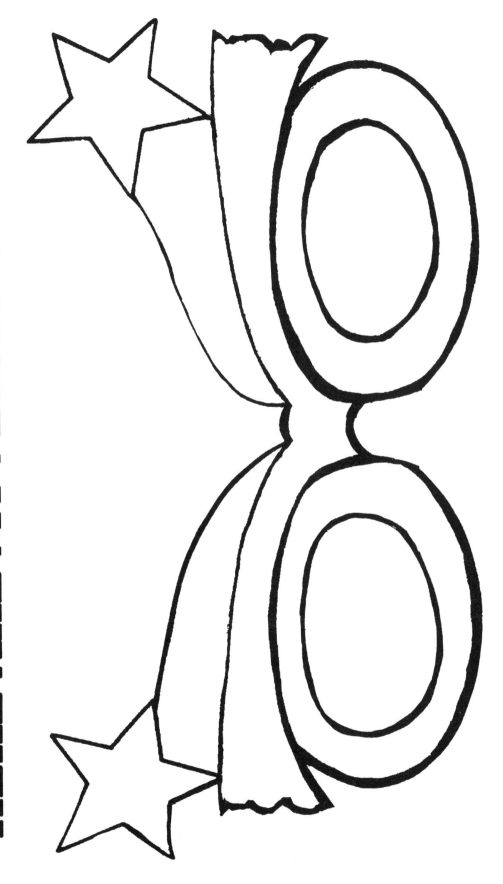

THE SAD HEART

MY SAD HEART STORY

_____

_____

_____

_____

_____

_____

_____

_____

_____

_____

_____

_____

_____

_____

by _____

MY HEART

3–40. MY FEELINGS RUN DEEP
3–41. HERE'S HOW MY FEELINGS RUN DEEP

Objective:

Children learn how to put themselves in the other person's place when hurt to develop feelings of *empathy*.

Materials Needed:

- "My Feelings Run Deep" and "Here's How My Feelings Run Deep" activity sheets
- *optional:* paper; stapler for booklet

Directions:

1. Ask your children to think about a recent time they saw someone hurt physically or emotionally. After they recall an incident, ask them to remember *how they felt* for the person who was hurt. Write the term "empathy" on the board and explain that it means they put themselves in the place of the person who is hurt and feel sorry for that person.

2. Take time to share stories from children about times when they felt sorry for someone who was hurt. As the stories are told, children will get the idea of what it means to have empathy for others. Some children do not understand what it means to put themselves in someone else's place and to feel sorry for them, so this will be a valuable introduction for them.

3. Pass "My Feelings Run Deep" activity sheets to students. The story, "Laughing at Lee," can be role-played in two scenes. The first scene is played out with Lee being humiliated as in the activity sheet. Then another scene should follow with two or three students helping Lee after he is made fun of and falls down. It is up to the students to make up the dialogue and gestures (arm around shoulder or a pat on the back) for this follow-up scene. Role-plays should be rehearsed before being performed for the class.

4. Have a class discussion about how Lee felt after the kids made fun of him. *Response:* "Lee's head was low so the other kids couldn't see he was ready to cry. He was so embarrassed! If I'd been him, I would have felt so humiliated!"

5. Point out that Lee's story has a double put-down because not only is Lee made fun of, but Lee's mom is also ridiculed for the way she dresses. Ask students how they think that put-down made Lee feel. *Response:* "Having your mom put-down really hurts. Lee probably felt worse hearing bad things about his mom than he felt about his own put-downs."

6. Give students the opportunity to volunteer what they would have done to make Lee feel better if they had witnessed this scene. *Responses:* "I would go up to him and offer to take him inside to fix up his skinned knee." "I'd tell him to forget about what the kids said and maybe that's the way they try to act big by putting others down." "I'd ask my Mom to donate some clothes to our school to privately give to his family."

7. Direct students' attention to their activity sheets to answer the questions either individually or together as a class.

"Here's How My Feelings Run Deep" Booklet:

Pass out "Here's How My Feelings Run Deep" as pages for booklets to be made by children after keeping track of their feelings for others. They are to take notes about their feelings when they see others hurt. You may want to give them a period of two or three weeks to observe others and to try to put themselves in their places when others are hurt. Taking notes and then writing their feelings down helps to teach children empathy for others. Before the booklet is due, students' notes could be printed on the computer for the final draft. Pages are attached to the cover page and bound together with blue yarn for a booklet.

Bulletin Board Link:

A deep-sea theme on blue background with fish made of gold foil features students' goggles displayed with the caption "My Feelings Run Deep" or "'Sea' Our World of Feelings."

MY FEELINGS RUN DEEP

Read the "Laughing at Lee" story below. We need to put ourselves in someone else's shoes and see the problem from his or her point of view. We then feel *empathy* for the person who is hurt—the *victim*. Think how you would feel if you were in Lee's shoes.

Laughing at Lee

Lee is wearing pants that are too short for him. His single mom is out of work and she can't afford to buy him new pants. Chelsea and Sam laugh at him at recess. Chelsea says, "Lee, you look so geeky! Are those pants your little sister's? Did your mom buy them at the Second Hands Clothes Store where she probably gets her clothes, too?" Chelsea and Sam laugh harder as Lee hangs his head low and wishes all the kids listening would disappear. A few of the kids standing around start making fun of Lee's mom's clothes. Lee runs away from the laughter. He tries hard not to let anybody see him start to cry. As he runs he trips and falls down, ripping his pants and skinning his knee. This makes the kids laugh even harder at him.

1. How would you feel if you had been in Lee's shoes and teased for your clothes? _____

   _____

2. How would Lee feel after this happened? _____

   _____

3. How do you feel about the way Lee was treated at recess? _____

   _____

4. What would you do to make Lee feel better? _____

   _____

5. Write on the back of this sheet about a time you saw someone hurt by others and how you would handle it now. _____

   _____

Name _____

HERE'S HOW MY FEELINGS RUN DEEP

Name _____

3–42. OOPS! WILBERT PUT HIS FOOT IN HIS MOUTH

Objective:

Students can relate to the "sticky situations" Wilbert experiences. Learning how to speak calmly and assertively in tense situations is a life skill students will use frequently. *Empathy* for the feelings of others is also an intended outcome of this activity.

Materials Needed:

- "Oops! Wilbert Put His Foot in His Mouth" activity sheet
- *Optional:* props for role-plays

Directions:

1. As you distribute the activity sheets, students will be amused to see their old friend, Wilbert, with his foot stuck in his mouth! Ask if they are familiar with the meaning of the phrase, "I've put my foot in my mouth!" *Responses:* "I've said the wrong thing!" "I've said something to embarrass someone else—or myself!"

2. Choose a student to read the activity introduction at the top of the sheet, explaining how Wilbert always seems to say the wrong thing during "sticky situations" or times of conflict. Ask, "How many of you can relate to Wilbert by sometimes saying the wrong thing in a 'sticky situation'?" *Responses:* Most hands will probably go up! Assure students that it is natural to make some mistakes at times, especially when we are faced with a conflict in which we feel emotionally upset.

3. You may choose to use the activity sheet as a whole-class activity, having each of the four "sticky situations" read aloud as students choose the better responses for each, followed by the role-plays. Or you may prefer to assign students the roles and play them out after the class finishes individually filling-in the better responses. Students will enjoy the humorous names and the way Wilbert gets himself into trouble in the "sticky situations." *Sticky situations answers:* 1. B; 2. C; 3. D; 4. A.

4. Review the term *empathy*. After writing the term on a chart or the board, explain that empathy is "the ability to share in another's emotions or feelings."

Language Arts Link:

Students may enjoy an extension of this activity by making "Sticky Situations" journals in which they record personal incidents they have had similar to Wilbert's, accompanied by drawings of the incidents, if desired. Students should include how they responded *before* this activity to the situations and how they would *now* respond with empathy for the feelings of others while expressing themselves calmly. Students' creative titles are encouraged. *Examples:* "Journal of My Stickiest Situations," "Unmentionables Now Told," or "No-Fail Ways to Turn Your Face Red!"

OOPS! WILBERT PUT HIS FOOT IN HIS MOUTH

Wilbert can't seem to say the right thing in "sticky situations" or times of conflict. When he's upset, he doesn't stop to think before he speaks. He blurts out angry words, putting his "foot in his mouth," or saying the wrong thing. Of course, then the conflict only gets worse! Help Wilbert find the right way to approach a disagreement. Put the correct words *right* into Wilbert's mouth by putting the letter of the answer you choose for Wilbert under the STICKY SITUATION. Your goal is for both persons involved in the conflict to feel happy with Wilbert's new knack of saying the *right* thing! Role-play the sticky situations first using the wrong methods, then role-play the same situations using the conflict-resolution skills you have learned.

1. **STICKY SITUATION:**

   Wilbert dropped his pencil during an English test and his teacher, Mrs. Sharpeyes, asked him suspiciously what he was doing. "It's not fair! You thought I was cheating, didn't you, Mrs. Sharpeyes?" Wilbert then received a lecture.

   A BETTER RESPONSE: _____

2. **STICKY SITUATION:**

   Wilbert's mom came home to find him watching TV. What she didn't know was he had completed his homework after school and had just sat down to watch TV. "Wilbert, turn off that TV and study!" his mom said. "I can't even relax around here! You're so mean to me!" Wilbert shouted and ran to his bedroom.

   A BETTER RESPONSE: _____

3. **STICKY SITUATION:**

   Wilbert asked Sandy Beach when her birthday was because he was nosy about whether she was 12 yet. She thought it meant he wanted to buy her a gift! When Wilbert found out, he blurted out, "Sandy, I just wanted to know how old you are because you look a lot younger than 12, and not so I could buy you something. I don't even like you, really!" Sandy's face turned red from embarrassment.

   A BETTER RESPONSE: _____

4. STICKY SITUATION:

Injured with a sprained ankle after he slipped on a banana peel at recess, Wilbert shouted loudly at Ian Ocent, who happened to be carrying a lunchbox, "Hey! Haven't you heard of throwing your leftovers into the trash bin? You'll be sorry for this accident!" Ian Ocent had not dropped the peel. He then got angry with Wilbert, followed by a fight which left Wilbert with a swollen eye.

A BETTER RESPONSE: _____

Help Wilbert with Better Responses He Could Have Chosen:

A. "Next time I'll watch where I'm heading! Could someone help? 'I've fallen and I can't get up' as the saying goes!"

B. "I was picking up my pencil which I dropped."

C. "I changed my routine and did my studying right after school today, before the TV time we agreed I could watch every day. You had no way of knowing because you were at work."

D. "Hey, it's cool you have a birthday in May. I just wondered if you'd turned 12 yet."

5. Make up your own sticky situation below:

_____

_____

_____

_____

_____

3–43. MY LISTENING MIRROR

Objective:

Primary students learn reflective listening or "mirroring" so both involved in a conflict feel they are listened to.

Materials Needed:

- "My Listening Mirror" activity sheet
- Colored markers; scissors; crayons; glitter; stickers
- *optional:* silver foil; paste
- *optional:* laminating equipment or clear self-stick vinyl
- lined paper; tape

Directions:

1. Ask children what they see when they look into a mirror. *Responses:* "I see myself making funny faces." "I see my reflection." Write the word "reflection" on the board. This will not be a difficult word for children to learn and many will already be familiar with it. Acknowledge that the images they see of themselves in mirrors are *reflections* or their images coming back to them. Tell them in this activity they are going to be doing some reflections, but not in a real mirror. Explain that they are going to reflect another person's words!

2. Pass activity sheets to students. They will be anxious to decorate and cut out their mirrors. Have stickers, glitter, and other supplies ready for children to use. After mirrors are decorated and names written on each child's mirror, try to laminate them so they can be used by the children often. Their mirrors will be used when they get into a conflict with someone else and need to write the words of the other person on the mirror. This writing gives them practice listening to someone else. Tell them not to forget it will then be their turn to be listened to!

3. Lined paper cut to the size of the inside of the mirrors should be made available in a "conflict-resolution corner." Each time a child wishes to use his or her mirror, a new piece of paper is taped onto the laminated mirrors for each new conflict.

Bulletin Board Link:

One large mirror lined with silver foil is displayed with the "rules" of mirroring inside:

> 1. **In a conflict, we listen to the other person.**
> 2. **We write what the other wants to happen.**
> 3. **We solve our problem so we are both happy.**

Captions are "We Mirror Each Other's Words" or "Looking at a Problem from the Other's View." Children's mirrors are hung in a place easily accessible for their use when they want to practice reflective listening.

MY LISTENING MIRROR

Decorate and cut out your mirror. When you have a conflict with somebody, take turns *mirroring* each other. Write their words about what they want to happen so both of you are happy with the solution. Remember to write the *other person's* words; not *your* words. Then read them back to the other person. Then it's your turn to be mirrored.

3–44. DELUXE PIZZA TOPPINGS

Objective:

Children learn to communicate using sayings that work in a conflict so everybody feels like a winner.

Materials Needed:

- "Deluxe Pizza Toppings" activity sheet
- Scissors; markers; crayons; paste
- *optional:* light brown, red, green, yellow, and white paper; paste

Directions:

1. Deliver pizzas to your class—the activity sheets, that is! This activity is a fun and creative way to teach communication in conflicts. If children have learned what to say when they have a conflict, they will be more apt to use these "phrases" when they are angry instead of swearing or hitting.

2. Brainstorm with your students the phrases they need to have ready the next time they have a conflict with someone. Ask what they like to hear someone say to them when they are angry. Write the phrases on the board as the children give them to you. *Responses:* "I want to solve this with you . . ." "I hear you telling me . . ."

3. Ask for phrases that turn them off to solving the conflict with the other person. *Responses:* "*You* are the one who started this!" "You're wrong; I'm right about this." "I'm going to get even!"

4. Students are to choose the sayings on the activity sheet that are the best to use so everybody feels like a winner. Have them write the numbers of the sayings they choose inside the pizza toppings. Point out and discuss that some of the sayings should *not* be used in a conflict because they only make the other person angrier and less likely to want to work out the problem. *Answers:* 1, 3, 4, 5, 7, 9.

5. After the numbers are written in the pizza toppings, students cut out the pizzas and paste inside the pizza boxes on the next page and fold the top over the pizzas. Children think of creative names for their pizza delivery and have fun decorating their pizza boxes.

Bulletin Board Link:

Students' pizza activity sheets are displayed so the tops can be opened and closed in order to see all the box designs. The caption is "We Use Deluxe Sayings in Our Conflicts." Or students make pizzas on light brown paper and cut them out. Their favorite qualities about themselves are written inside the toppings they make, cut out, and pasted on their pizzas. The caption is "Any Way You Slice It, We're Deluxe!"

DELUXE PIZZA TOPPINGS

Choose from the numbers below the things to say when you want to solve a problem so everybody is a winner. Write those numbers in the pizza toppings on the pizza below. Cut out the pizza then paste it in the box and fold it over your pizza. Create a name and design for your pizza delivery service!

1. Let's try to work this out . . .

2. You loser!

3. Nobody will feel like a loser if we . . .

4. Let's think of some ways . . .

5. When you yell, I feel upset . . .

6. That's not the way I'd do it.

7. I hear you saying . . .

8. You're wrong!

9. I'm tuning in to hear your side . . .

10. You shouldn't have . . .

DELUXE PIZZA TOPPINGS (continued)

3–45. HEY, STOP BEING PUSHY!

Objective:

Children learn the difference between nice but firm (assertive) and pushy or annoying (aggressive) behavior that nobody likes.

Materials Needed:

- "Hey, Stop Being Pushy" activity sheet
- Masking tape

Directions:

1. To introduce this activity, make a line on the floor with masking tape. Tell your class this line is to demonstrate people who *cross the line* in getting what they want. Ask for a volunteer to give an example of someone who acts pushy to get his or her way. Ask the volunteer to stand at the tape and to cross the line while explaining how he or she is acting pushy.

2. Write the terms "assertive" and "aggressive" on the board. Read students the following story as an example to demonstrate pushy (aggressive) and firm but fair (assertive) behavior.

I JUST NEED A LITTLE HELP! (WHEN *I'M* READY, THAT IS!)

Fred asks you to help him on the computer for just five minutes right after school today. You agree to meet him as soon as the bell rings. Your Mom had told you to come home right after school. You have an appointment at your dentist, but you know you can make it easily if you meet Fred right after school. You wait 15 minutes after school and Fred does not show up. You worry you'll miss your appointment at the dentist. Just as you are starting to leave, he shows up nearly 20 minutes late. You say you have another appointment and cannot stay to help after all because it is too late. He tries to talk you into staying to show him just a couple of "how-to's" on the computer. He says it will only take you a minute. You picture yourself rushing home and then having to wait at the dentist's office because you were late and they took the next patient. You decide to make your needs nicely but firmly known to Fred. You tell him you have to leave right now and you will help him another day when you do not have an appointment.

3. Ask students when they felt Fred "crossed the line" and became too pushy or aggressive. *Response:* "He crossed the line and got too pushy when he showed up late and still expected help on the computer! He was only thinking of his own needs and getting his own way. He wasn't thinking of the other person who needed to get to an appointment on time." Ask if they felt the other's needs were made in a nice but firm way in order to meet the need of getting to the dentist's appointment on time. *Response:* "I think Fred got the point in a good way. I don't think he will be late again!"

4. Pass out the activity sheets and point out the two ways in the scenario that show children behavior people may use to get what they want. **Get Out of My Way!** ***The pushy (aggressive) way:*** They may get what they want in a pushy way that ends up with

someone feeling hurt. **I Need to Be Able to See!** *The firm (assertive) way:* They may get what they want firmly but nicely so that nobody feels hurt.

5. Have students read and volunteer to role-play the *pushy* scenario, *Get Out of My Way!* Ask how they feel about Lyn's behavior. *Response:* She was too pushy. Kids don't like to be around somebody like Lyn."

6. Have students read and volunteer to role-play the next scenario, *I Need to Be Able to See!* Ask how students feel about the way Tim handled Lyn's pushing ahead in line. *Response:* "He stood up for his right because he was in line before Lyn was. Otherwise, he wouldn't have been able to see the play very well." Describe Tim's behavior as firm or assertive.

7. Depending on the ages of your students, discuss the questions together or have them completed individually. Ask them for other ways *Get Out of My Way!* could be solved. Discuss with students the importance of making their needs known in a nice but firm (assertive) way while considering the needs of others.

Name _____

HEY, STOP BEING PUSHY!

If you got something you wanted but somebody ended up feeling hurt, then you had been too "pushy" or *aggressive.* Do you enjoy being around pushy people? Not many people do! Learning to get what you want nicely but firmly so nobody is hurt is being *assertive.* Role-play these skits.

Aggressive Skit: Get Out of My Way!

Kids are in line for an awesome play in the gym. Lyn wants to be in the front of the line to get a good seat. Pushing ahead of the other kids in line, she says, "Get out of my way!" She gets to be first in line. Some of the smaller kids will now be seated behind Lyn, who is tall for her age.

Assertive Skit: I Need to be Able to See!

Tim (sometimes called "tiny Tim" because he is short for his age) gets really annoyed when Lyn pushes her way ahead of him to the front of the line. He looks right at Lyn and says, "Hey, I need to be at the front of the line, Lyn, so I can see the play. I was here in line first and I want you to move behind me as well as the shorter kids in line so you won't block our view."

1. How did Lyn get to be in front of the line for a good seat? _____

   _____

2. How did others get hurt by Lyn's actions? _____

   _____

3. Do you agree with how Tim made his needs known? _____ Why or why

   not? _____

   _____

4. Do you like to be with pushy kids? _____ Why or why not? _____

   _____

5. Do you think you are usually assertive or aggressive in order to get what you

   want? _____ Explain your answer. _____

   _____

© 1998 by The Center for Applied Research in Education

3–46. TWISTED TALES

Objective:

Misunderstanding, or faulty restating of another's words, often causes conflict. Students practice skills of clear communication and accurate listening that are helpful in avoiding being misunderstood by others.

Materials Needed:

- "Twisted Tales" activity sheet
- Paper for humorous stories
- Brown colored pencils; scissors

Directions:

1. Ask how many of your students have had times when something they have said to someone else came back to them totally different; we could say it was "twisted" from what they really said. Most hands will probably go up. Volunteers can share some of their "twisted tales" and how they felt when their original stories were changed. Responses will vary, but most students will say they do not feel good about their communication being misunderstood. This will open up discussion about ways they can avoid having their words twisted or twisting what others say to them.

2. Discuss the reasons words come back to us differently from the original intent. *Responses:* "The communicator might not make herself or himself clearly understood." "The person listening doesn't pay enough attention and gets it all mixed up." "The person hears the story from somebody else and tells it to others, changing the story to get the person in trouble, like when rumors start." "The listener just doesn't understand what the person says."

3. Pass the "Twisted Tales" activity sheet to your students to share their own mixed-up communication times on the twisted-tales cards. You may choose to have one card with an actual experience they have had and the other card with a fun twisted tale they make up.

4. After they have had time to complete their tales, students can have the option of choosing one tale for role-playing with others. After you have checked their choices to role-play, allow time for short rehearsals. The role-plays may then be enjoyed by the class so that children will realize the importance of clear communication skills while speaking and listening.

Listening Game:

1. Divide your class into two or three groups (or more groups if preferred for larger primary classes) and ask them to sit down after forming circles.

2. Choose one person to start the sentences, the number of which will be determined by the ages of your students. Choose sentence combinations according to the ages and abilities of your students. Use as few or as many sentences you think your students can

remember. Or make up your own sentences or have students take turns inventing sentence combinations. For younger students or special groups, you may choose to use portions of the sentences given later which offer a few ideas to get started.

3. Each child passes the sentence(s) on to the next child by whispering in the child's ear.

4. Children continue to whisper sentence(s) to the next person.

5. When the last person in the circle has heard the sentence(s), he or she repeats the sentence(s) aloud to the person sitting next to him or her who began the sentence(s).

6. The last child asks the beginner if this was what the original sentence was. If sentences were repeated correctly, congratulate the group on their communication skills. If the sentences got "twisted" or completely lost their original meaning, without singling out any child in the circle, review the communication skill of listening carefully to what the person is saying and repeating it, in this case, not to the person who spoke but to the next person. (**Note**: The circles are *not* in competition for this game so no one is pointed out as having "messed up" the sentences.)

> Choose sentence combinations according to the ages and abilities of your students. Use as few or as many sentences you think your students can remember. Or make up your own sentences or have students take turns inventing sentence combinations. For younger students or special groups, you may choose to use portions of the sentences given later which offer a few ideas to get started.

7. Sentences for Listening Game Topic #1: "Phone in to Pizza with Pizazz":

   Pete Piazza prefers pepperoni pizza with pineapple.

   Pete's friend, Anna, adores pizza with anchovies.

   Anna's friend, Lotsa, likes everything-on-it pizzas.

   Lotsa's friend, Cheesey, loves double-cheese pizzas.

   Cheesey's friend, Dorky, must have ooey-gooey pizzas.

8. Sentences for Listening Game Topic #2: "Homer's Horrible Headache":

   Homer forgot his Math homework and said it fell in a puddle.

   Homer told his teacher the puddle was muddy and made his Math murky.

   Homer's teacher, Mr. Unamused, told him to stay in at recess.

   At recess, Homer said he would work to "unmurk" his Math.

   The principal, Mrs. Stayover, told Homer to do his Math over or stay after school.

Language Arts Link:

Students can have fun making up some humorous "twisted tales." They can draw a huge pretzel on a page and inside the pretzel tell a story in which something someone said got terribly twisted and so out-of-hand that it had catastrophic results! If they have more than one humorous tale, students can cut out their pages in the shapes of pretzels and form booklets with a cover page and a creative title of their choosing.

TWISTED TALES

Have you ever been misunderstood? Has something you did or said gotten so twisted that there was a communication mix-up and not what you really meant at all? Inside the pretzel cards below, write about some experiences you've had that got twisted.

3–47. HEY! WHAT'S *REALLY* GOING ON?

Objective:

Children realize the anger they display at times is not really about the present issue. This activity explores *what is really behind* their angry behavior when an unresolved past issue "haunts" them.

Materials Needed:

- "Hey! What's *Really* Going On?" activity sheet
- Pens; markers

Directions:

1. Pass out activity sheets to students, explaining that sometimes we confuse unsolved issues or problems in our pasts with present problems. Introduce the phrase "haunted by the past." Write the following words on the board and discuss each point, all of which answer the question. "What's *really* happening here?"

   ISSUES—What are the problems that need to be solved about the issue right now? Is there underlying anger about an issue that happened before, a "ghost" of a past conflict?

   COMMUNICATIONS—Are you giving each other enough information about your feelings and needs with respect to the conflict now? Are you sure you are not dealing with a past conflict? What kind of body language are you giving? Closed body language—crossed arms or legs, or your eyes or body positioned away from your partner, along with frowns or scowls, can "haunt" your best oral conflict-resolving efforts!

   PERSONAL FEELINGS—Are you dealing with angry or hurt feelings about this present conflict or are your feelings really about a past conflict? Are you expressing your feelings openly and honestly?

2. Ask for children to recount a conflict they have had and, looking back, reacted not to the issue at hand but to something that happened *in the past.* You may want to give an example of your own (which we all have!) as a starter. *Response:* "I screamed at my friend when she didn't return the video to the video store on time. She really couldn't help it because her mom had to work late so she drove her to the store and got the video in late. What I was *really* angry about was something that happened last week. I got a late fine from the library because she didn't give my book back I had loaned her three weeks before. I realize now I blew up about something that haunted me and I didn't know it at the time!"

HEY! WHAT'S *REALLY* GOING ON?

Sometimes we feel angry with somebody about not just what happens NOW; we are still angry about something that happened BEFORE! Then we blow up about something that is really small because we're still mad about what happened in the past. We can say we are *haunted* by a past issue because it stays with us, ready to appear again like a ghost! When you feel angry, try to remember to focus on the issue at hand and not the past.

Think about a time you got really mad at somebody over something small, but after you thought about it, you were still mad about something else he or she did before. Write about it below.

Name _____

3–48. SCRAMBLED EGGS

Objective:

Children review the importance of listening to the other person in a conflict.

Materials Needed:

- "Scrambled Eggs" activity sheet
- *optional:* colored eggs; paste; paper

Directions:

1. Children will see the comic figure of Wilbert when they receive their activity sheets. Explain that they are going to unscramble Wilbert's scrambled eggs to spell a message. They should remember to do this so everyone feels like a winner in a conflict. *Give them the clue:* "The word is found in one of the TLC steps." Refer to the TLC steps on a poster you may have or write the steps on the board for review with your class. (The answer to unscrambling the scrambled eggs is: **Listen**.)

2. Discuss listening together. Ask for volunteers to discuss how they feel when they are talking and not being listened to. *Response:* "I feel angry when I talk and the person I'm talking to doesn't pay attention to me!" Ask how many of them think about what they are going to say next instead of listening to the person speaking to them. *Response:* "I think more about what I'm going to say than what the person is telling me." Remind them to remember how they feel when they aren't listened to next time they are in the role of listener.

3. Direct the students' attention to the two eggs at the bottom of the activity sheet that are called *eggs-pectations.* In the first egg, they are to write how they expect somebody will listen to them the next time they have a conflict. In the second egg, they will write about how they will listen to that person.

Art and Bulletin Board Link:

Have fun with eggshell art with your class. Have children remove shells from colored hard-boiled eggs. They crush the shells and create their own designs to glue to colorful backgrounds. You may want to have students form "TLC" with their eggshells for a colorful TLC display. The caption is "We Have TLC Eggs-Pectations!"

SCRAMBLED EGGS

Wilbert dropped the eggs out of the container he was carrying when he was trying to find the message in them. Help Wilbert unscramble the letters in the eggs below. The letters will spell a message to remember when you are solving a conflict so everyone feels like a winner. (*Clue:* The word is found in one of the TLC steps.)

— — — — — — —

In the first egg below tell how you *expect* somebody will listen to you and in the second egg how you *expect* to listen to him or her the next time you have a conflict. Call these your EGGS-PECTATIONS!

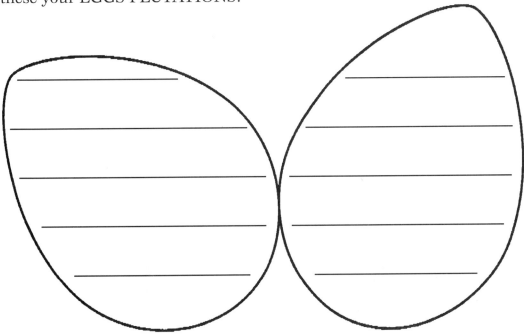

3–49. MUMBO JUMBO SOUP

Objective:

Children learn nobody can make them feel low if they don't let them.

Materials Needed:

- "Mumbo Jumbo Soup" activity sheet
- Colored markers; pens

Directions:

1. Children will enjoy the activity sheets as you pass them out and they see the comic figure, Wilbert, getting himself into another predicament! They will read at the top of the sheet that this time he dropped his bowl of soup and it went everywhere. Ask students how they think Wilbert felt. *Response:* "Wilbert probably felt really embarrassed when he fell down in front of his customers and his soup spilled all over the place."

   This response can lead to a class discussion about embarrassment and who is responsible for making us feel low about ourselves. Ask for volunteers to share their own stories of times they were embarrassed and low and to tell about how they handled their feelings. *Response:* "One time my teacher called on me and I wasn't paying attention so I gave an answer that was totally wrong. One of the kids called me stupid and I *felt so stupid* that I could feel my face getting red!"

2. The discussion on embarrassment will lead to your asking your class the following question: "Who made each of you who had embarrassing experiences feel low about yourselves?" The responses will vary but they will invariably name others for making them feel low about themselves. Lead students to the realization that although others may do something that causes them to feel embarrassed, *they* are the ones who ultimately decide if they will allow themselves to feel low about themselves.

   This is an especially important lesson for children who are constantly ridiculed or put down at home with comments such as: "You'll never amount to anything." "You're just no good." "You're bad." "You'll never get good grades like your brother gets." "You're not athletically inclined." If children do not receive some positive comments outside the home, they may never be aware of any positive qualities they possess.

   Children need to be taught *they* are the ones who allow any put-downs they receive to have a negative effect on them. *Example:* If they are told over and over that they are "stupid" and they allow themselves to believe it and to feel inferior to others, it will become self-fulfilling. On the other hand, even though they receive lots of negativity in their lives, they can "rise above" it and believe in themselves; they *can* do the thing they were told they cannot do!

3. After the class discussion, ask students to find the message on the alphabet noodles that Wilbert spilled. *The message is:* **Nobody can make you feel low about yourself if *you* don't let them.** Students fill in the words "you," "let" and "them."

4. Write the message on the board and have it hanging on display in your classroom all year to remind children of this quotation by Eleanor Roosevelt: "No one can make you feel inferior without your consent."

5. At the bottom of the activity sheet ask students to write about a time they felt low about themselves and what they would do now (after this lesson) if it happened again. When the bottom of the sheets are completed, ask for volunteers to share what they wrote with the class. *Responses:* "In the past kids have made fun of me when I've been up to bat and taunted me about all the strike-outs I make. I'm not going to think negatively next time. I'll think, I CAN get a hit!" "Kids make fun of me and tell me I'm fat. Now I see I am *letting them* make me feel low. They won't get to me anymore."

MUMBO JUMBO SOUP

Wilbert was carrying a big bowl of soup for his customers to try at his restaurant. But he tripped on a banana peel and his customers laughed at Wilbert as the soup went all over the place! He felt so embarrassed! He'd made the soup with alphabet noodles and he saw a message they spelled that he will try to remember whenever people laugh at him. Can you put the spilled letters together to fill in this message for him?

Nobody can make you feel low about yourself if _____ don't _____ _____ .

© 1998 by The Center for Applied Research in Education

M

Y   H

T

E

O

U   T

E   L

Write about a time you felt low about yourself and what you would do now if it happened again.

_____

_____

_____

_____

_____

_____

3–50. A GEEKY PLAY

Objective:

Students learn that they are who they believe they are—not who someone else tells them they are. This is an enjoyable skit that leaves a lasting impression as students recall the humorous scenario between Wilbert and Granny.

Materials Needed:

- "A Geeky Play" activity sheet
- Role-play props: large brimmed hat with a flower and yardstick to use as Granny's cane; "geeky" goggles or sunglasses; crazy scarf, tie, or hat

Directions:

1. Decide who you would like to play the roles of "Granny" and "Wilbert" in the skit. Reversal of the male and female roles is recommended. Students find it lots of fun to see a boy play the role of "Granny." They laugh when he hobbles in wearing a big flowered hat! They also find it funny to see a girl play the role of "Wilbert." Wilbert enters wearing something "geeky," such as goggles atop his head or strange sunglasses along with a loud scarf, tie, or hat. It's a good idea to privately ask the two students you choose to play the roles if they would enjoy taking the parts. Some children love the fun of playing a character of the opposite sex; others find it embarrassing.

2. Students who are chosen and have agreed to play the roles should take their props and practice their lines outside the classroom. This way, the whole skit will be a surprise to the rest of the class. It isn't necessary for students to memorize their lines. Reading their lines from their activity sheets, which may be given to them but not to the class before they have seen the skit, or from role-play cards as they present the skit, works well. When they are ready, introduce the skit to your students by announcing you would like them to welcome a couple of visitors to your classroom, a Granny and her grandson, Wilbert! Students will recognize the name "Wilbert" from the comical recurring character they see on their activity sheets.

3. Because the skit ends on a more serious note than it began, it may be necessary for you to initiate the applause and keep the enthusiasm for the students who performed high by congratulating them on being "good sports" by changing their genders for the skit!

4. Pass out the activity sheets to your students to process the intended outcome of the skit. Review with them the following concepts:
   - Nobody can make you feel low if you don't let them.
   - You are in charge of your own reactions to an event:

     $E + R = O$ (Event + Response = Outcome)
   - You are what you believe you are; not what someone else tells you you are.

The questions at the bottom of the activity sheet enable children to relate to a time they were put down and to express the way they felt. The aim is that their replies to the questions reveal the understanding of the concept that *they are in charge of who they believe they are; not who someone else tells them they are.* Ask students to fill out the bottom of their sheets individually. Discuss their answers together.

A GEEKY PLAY

Role play: Are You a Geek or a Lotus?

Granny enters first, hobbling in with her "cane" or "walker" in front of her, wearing a fancy hat. Wilbert follows, wearing goggles above his head or sunglasses and a crazy tie, scarf, or hat. Granny speaks first.

GRANNY: "Why are you so upset, Wilbert?"

Wilbert: "Because Tony called me a geek and now I feel like such a geek!"

Granny: "Well, Wilbert, why don't you believe you're a Lotus?"

Wilbert: "Man! No offense, Granny, but I think you're losing it!! You think I'm a race car??"

Granny: "Wilbert, if you believe you're a geek just because Tony called you a geek, you might as well believe you are a shiny race car—a LOTUS."

Wilbert: "Hey, I'm getting it, Granny. I'm what *I* think I am—NOT what someone else tells me I am!"

GRANNY: "I'll remember that, Wilbert. I KNOW I'm not losing it, even though *I* was told I was losing it—by *somebody*!"

WILBERT: "Stay cool, Granny!"

Write your responses to the following questions.

1. Have you ever felt like Wilbert did when he was called a geek? If so, write about how you felt.

   _____

   _____

   _____

2. What did you think of the advice Granny gave Wilbert?

   _____

   _____

   _____

3. What's a good rule for how you're going to react now if someone puts you down?

   _____

   _____

   _____

© 1998 by The Center for Applied Research in Education

3–51. CONFLICT CANDY BARS

Objective:

Children give their solutions in candy bars for everyday conflict situations that involve choices between honesty and dishonesty.

Materials Needed:

- "Conflict Candy Bar" activity sheets
- Scissors
- Markers; pens
- *optional:* gold or silver foil
- laminating equipment or clear self-stick vinyl

Directions:

1. Prepare the candy bars by cutting each and laminating for future use. Mount them on silver or gold foil for added appeal. Have many copies to keep at your conflict-solving or creative problem-solving center in your classroom.

2. Write the words "honesty" and "dishonesty" on the board. Ask for students to tell you what the words mean to them. *Responses:* "Honesty is when you tell the truth. It's when you don't lie, cheat, or steal." "Dishonesty means lying. A person lies when he or she doesn't want to tell the truth about something." Ask for volunteers to give examples of problems solved honestly and for examples of problems that were solved dishonestly. Discuss students' feelings about the two words.

3. Ask children if they would be honest even if they knew no one else would ever find out they did not tell the truth. *Responses:* "Maybe nobody else would know that I lied, but I would always know." "Something inside me would tell me that I did not tell the truth. I'd feel guilty." Explain that the "something inside me" is your *conscience* that bothers you if you don't do what you feel is right.

4. Cut out the conflict candy bars and divide your class into pairs. Pass a conflict candy bar to each pair. Ask each pair to first talk about how they would solve the conflict solution. Remind them of your discussion about honesty and to think about how to use it in their solutions. Each pair will then role-play their conflict with their solution.

5. Students enjoy making up their own conflict candy bars. Some blank conflict candy bars are included as an extra activity sheet. Ask students to write their conflicts on scrap paper before neatly copying their conflicts onto their candy bars. These can then be laminated and used for other children to solve.

CONFLICT CANDY BAR

Here's my conflict in a nutshell. My mom told me to load up one of her large fancy dishes with peanuts for the grownups she was having over. I did that. She told me to put our dog, Hoggit, outside. I didn't get around to doing that. I heard a munching sound and nearly flipped out as I ran as fast as I could to see what happened. I saw Hoggit had tipped the peanut dish over. All the peanuts were gone! Just then the dog got sick from the peanuts he'd gobbled up and the carpet was a mess! Mom was getting changed and called out from her bedroom, "How is it going?" I . . .

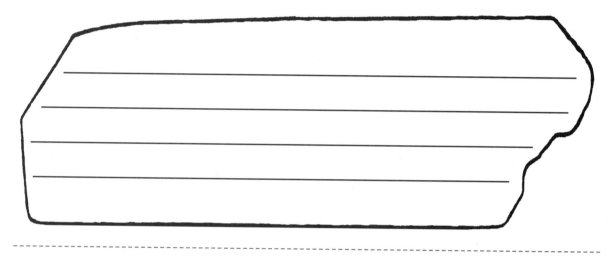

CONFLICT CANDY BAR

I knew I was in BIG trouble when I had secretly taped a TV show my Dad told me he did *not* want me to watch because he thought it had too much violence. Then I forgot to label the videotape. My dad picked it up and began to rewind it for a show he wanted to tape. He asked what was on it because it was not at the beginning of the tape! I had to decide whether to tell him what I did or just see if I"d get by with what *he may never find out.* I . . .

CONFLICT CANDY BAR

I'd had a bad day at school. It was one of those days when a whole lot of things went wrong. I forgot my lunch and had no money. I worked for an hour on Math and did a great job on the wrong page. Then I got the last strike-out for my team's baseball game. Finally, I mixed up the date of my History quiz that turned out to be today and was a total disaster! Chilling out on my bed at home my mom wants to know why I'm not studying for my History quiz. Do I tell her the quiz was today or hope she'll leave me alone and not find out? I . . .

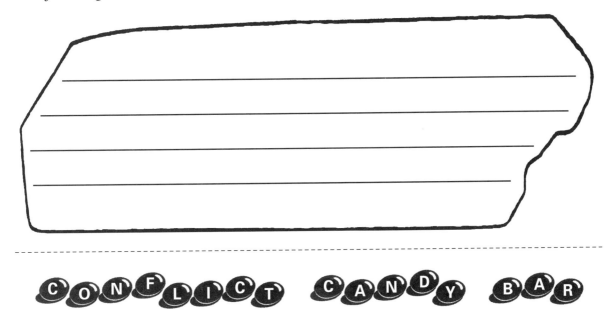

CONFLICT CANDY BAR

It all started when the phone rang. A message was left for my older sister, Ann, by her best friend, Lisa. You have to understand that Ann LIVES for her phone calls. I was sure I'd remember to give her the message. Ann came home the next day really angry at Lisa who would not speak to her all day and Ann didn't know why. Oops!! I remembered I forgot to tell her about the phone message! Ann and Lisa both say they are no longer friends. Since they aren't talking to each other any more, Ann may never find out *it was all my fault.* I . . .

CONFLICT CANDY BAR

Conflict: _____

_____

_____

Solution: _____

_____

_____

_____

- -

CONFLICT CANDY BAR

Conflict: _____

_____

_____

Solution: _____

_____

_____

_____

3–52. A RAINBOW OF PEACE

Objective:

Children learn that peace begins inside ourselves before we can spread it to others. Our "pot of gold" at the end of our conflicts is for both in the conflict to end up feeling peaceful.

Materials Needed:

- "A Rainbow of Peace" activity sheet
- Markers or crayons (violet, violet-blue, blue, green, yellow, orange, and red)
- *optional:* gold foil; black or gold paper; gold or brown pipe cleaners; pastel markers or chalk

Directions:

1. Discuss the children's experiences with rainbows. Take time to talk about the beauty of rainbows and the pleasure they give us. Explain that a rainbow is formed in the sky by the reflection of the sun's rays in falling rain or mist. You may want to use a prism to demonstrate the rainbow effect. Books with pictures of rainbows will give children who have never seen a rainbow the chance to see them. Ask children when to look for them in the sky. *Response:* "I saw a rainbow after it had just rained and the sun came out." Enjoy discussing the pretty colors of a rainbow that are violet, indigo (violet-blue), blue, green, yellow, orange, and red. Explain that these are the colors of a spectrum also known as the prismatic or primary colors named by Sir Isaac Newton.

2. Ask children *how they feel* when they have seen a real rainbow or viewed one in the prism or in pictures. *Responses:* "I felt calm just looking at the rainbow." "It felt peaceful looking at what was made by nature." When the words "calm" or "peaceful" are used, write the terms on the board and ask for other descriptions about feeling peaceful. *Responses:* "I feel like I don't have any problems." "Chilled out." "I don't have to feel worried or scared about anything." "Relaxed."

3. Ask children if they have heard the story that has been handed down for a long time and cannot be verified (a *legend*) about a pot of gold at the end of a rainbow. Many of your children will be familiar with this legend. Ask for a volunteer to explain the legend for those in the class who have not heard it. Discuss whether or not legends are true stories. *Response:* "Legends are often myths. We often like myths, like the pot of gold at the end of the rainbow, so we want to believe them. But they usually aren't true."

4. Pass out activity sheets. Ask students to look at a rainbow of peace to see that peace begins within themselves and is spread to others around them and then to the world. Beginning with band #1 of the rainbow, ask students to write about one thing they will do to make peace inside themselves. In band #2, they write one thing they will do to make peace toward others and in band #3, for making peace in the world.

5. In the pot of gold students are to write about how they handled a conflict with somebody that ended up with both of them feeling peaceful with each other.

6. After sheets are completed, ask volunteers to share and discuss together their peace comments from their rainbows and their "pot of gold" ideas.

Bulletin Board Link:

A large black paper pot of gold (with your class picture inside) is the focal point surrounded by students' individual pots of gold made from black or gold paper or foil. Gold or brown pipe cleaners may be used for pot handles. Inside the students' pots staple each child's pot of gold from the activity sheets with their feelings about peace at the end of their conflicts. The caption is "Search for Treasured Conflict Solvers" or "Discover the Secret Treasure of Solving Conflicts." In addition to—or instead of—the pots, display the students' rainbows from the activity sheets with their ideas to spread peace. All of their small rainbows could be placed together to form one large rainbow display. (If other classes complete this activity and combine their students' rainbows with yours, you could make one huge rainbow for a front hall display.) The caption is "(Name of school)'s Rainbow of Peace."

Name _____

A RAINBOW OF PEACE

Do you like to look for rainbows after it has rained and the sun comes out? Does a rainbow make you feel peaceful? The next time you look at a rainbow, think how *peace* begins inside ourselves. It continues when we spread peace to others. At the end of the rainbow, it is said there is a pot of gold. Write in the pot of gold below how you handled a conflict you had that ended up with both of you feeling peaceful with each other.

Write in the rainbow spaces how you will make: 1. Peace inside myself; 2. Peace with others around me; 3. Peace in the world.

1.

2.

3.

3–53. TLC POSTER
3–54. WILBERT'S RESTAURANT
3–55. STICKY SITUATION SKIT: EATING WITH RELISH!
3–56. STICKY SITUATION SKIT: MAD MO
3–57. WILBERT'S IN A PICKLE

Objective:

Children gain practice in thinking of creative ways to solve problems in fun situations.

Materials Needed:

- "Wilbert's Restaurant," "Sticky Situation Skit: Eating with Relish!" "Sticky Situation Skit: Mad Mo," and "Wilbert's in a Pickle" activity sheets
- TLC poster
- Props for skits: empty mustard and ketchup containers; hamburger buns; hamburgers made of brown paper or plasticine
- Colored markers; crayons; scissors

Directions:

1. Pass out a TLC poster for each student along with "Wilbert's Restaurant" activity sheets. As students become familiar with the character Wilbert, they will anticipate he will get himself into a problem in his new restaurant business. Discuss the phrase "sticky situations." Explain these are conflicts that are usually not of a serious nature, yet they usually involve someone in the conflict who has hurt feelings that can be helped if the sticky situation is handled well. Give an example of a sticky situation of your own that was a challenge to handle so that everybody won. Once students understand the idea of a sticky situation, give them an opportunity to share their own experiences. Have a good time with these examples if some of their experiences are humorous. Don't forget to share your own!

2. Review the TLC steps shown on your TLC poster: **T**une in to the other person's feelings; **L**isten to how the other sees the problem, then take turns repeating back the other's words; **C**hoose a solution to meet both persons' needs so everybody wins. Tell students to read each of the sticky situations on their activity sheets and to write their own solutions on separate sheets of paper so that everybody wins. Remind them when writing their solutions to use the TLC steps that are displayed in your classroom.

3. Choose students to role-play the sticky situations "Eating with Relish," "Mad Mo," and "Wilbert's in a Pickle." They will perform for the class after rehearsals. Scripts for the skits are on the activity sheets.

4. After each sticky situation is role-played, ask if students agree that winning solutions were chosen. Discuss together the solutions chosen in the skits performed by the class.

5. Tell students they can create their own sticky situation skits! They write their own skits in the center of the activity sheet under "My Sticky Situation." Children have fun

making up these skits while learning how to listen to the other person and to think of solutions in which they both win. They also enjoy making make up their own titles. They then role-play with partners how they would handle the sticky situation they created so everybody wins.

6. "Wilbert's Restaurant" may be cut out and the doors folded inward. Students may then enjoy decorating the doors so customers will want to come in to try Wilbert's awesome hamburgers!

Creative Link:

Announce to your class that Wilbert needs some marketing for his new restaurant. Students can create flyers, brochures, banners, and posters manually or with computers to spark interest for customers to come in to try his "awesome hamburgers." Older students could illustrate a plan of the tables, chairs, counter, grill, kitchen space, etc., and plans for an innovative drive-thru. They should be encouraged to create slogans and specials to attract people to Wilbert's new restaurant.

CHILL OUT!

Use the TLC approach to conflicts:

TUNE IN to both of your feelings by each taking turns telling your side of the problem.

LISTEN to how the other sees the problem, then take turns repeating back the other's words.

CHOOSE A SOLUTION to meet both persons' needs so both feel like winners.

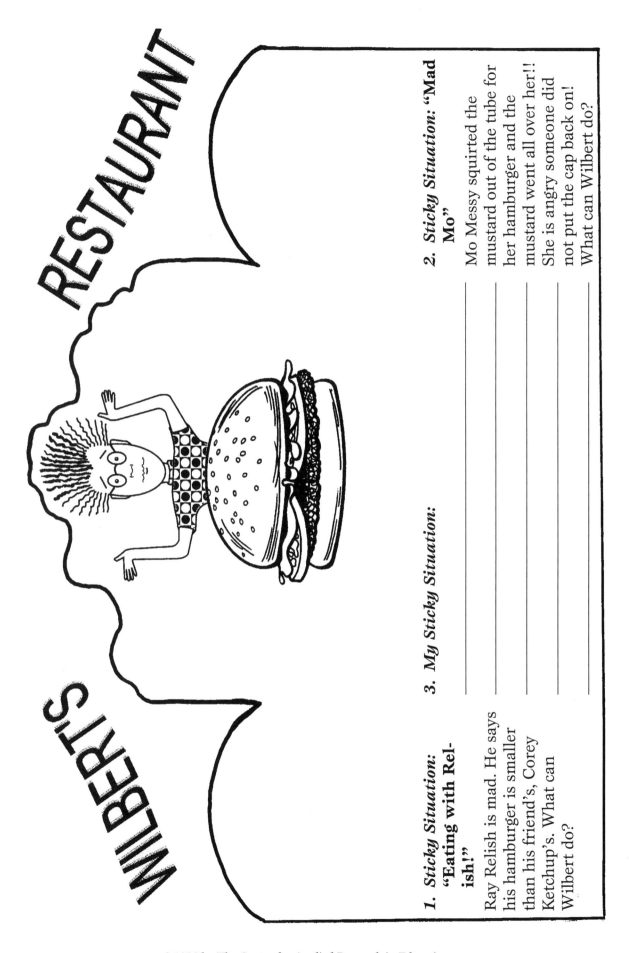

RESTAURANT

WILBERT'S

1. *Sticky Situation:* **"Eating with Relish!"**

Ray Relish is mad. He says his hamburger is smaller than his friend's, Corey Ketchup's. What can Wilbert do?

2. *Sticky Situation:* **"Mad Mo"**

Mo Messy squirted the mustard out of the tube for her hamburger and the mustard went all over her!! She is angry someone did not put the cap back on! What can Wilbert do?

3. *My Sticky Situation:*

_____
_____
_____
_____
_____
_____

STICKY SITUATIONS SKIT:"EATING WITH RELISH!"

NARRATOR: "Here's the sticky situation: Ray Relish sits down in Wilbert's Restaurant at a table next to Corey Ketchup's table. He is all excited to try these awesome hamburgers everyone is talking about ever since Wilbert opened his new restaurant. Ray has some money from his birthday and he is going to spend it here on a hamburger and a make-your-own-sundae with any flavor whipped cream you want! He plans to choose Wilbert's specialty that he makes himself called doubly decadent dynamite fudge! He calls Wilbert over to take his order."

RAY RELISH: "Hi, Wilbert! Nice place you have here. How's business?"

WILBERT: "Well, Ray, business is . . ."

RAY RELISH: *(Not listening to Wilbert's answer, he interrupts so he can hurry up and order.)* "Hey, Wilbert, how about an awesome burger? I've been saving my birthday money to spend here. I'm going to top it off with one of your sundaes at your make-your-own-sundae booth. How soon will that burger be here?"

WILBERT: "Coming right up, Ray. I just have to give Corey Ketchup her hamburger because she ordered first." *(Wilbert rushes to the kitchen and appears with Corey's hamburger.)*

COREY KETCHUP: "Thanks, Wilbert. What great service. This hamburger does look awesome. May I please have lots of ketchup? You know I love ketchup!" *(Wilbert gives her an extra container and she squirts it on her hamburger. Ray Relish is watching.)*

RAY RELISH: "Oh, Wilbert! Could you bring me some extra relish? I love to eat hamburgers with relish! Corey, you have a good-sized hamburger there. It looks great! I can't wait to get mine. *(Ray sees Wilbert coming to his table with the hamburger.)* Here it comes now. Y-Y-e-ss!"

WILBERT: "Here you go, buddy." *(He hands the plate to Ray.)*

RAY RELISH: *(He lifts up the hamburger bun and realizes his hamburger is smaller than he expected. He looks over at Corey's hamburger and is angry at Wilbert. His voice is angry.)* "Hey, man, this hamburger is smaller than Corey's. This isn't such an awesome burger!"

NARRATOR: "Wilbert isn't sure how to solve this problem. He figures all his hamburgers can't be exactly the same size, and he thinks it's not fair for his customers to expect that! But he also wants to keep Ray, a friend, coming back. He tries to look at the problem from Ray's hungry point of view! See what you think of the way Wilbert handles this problem."

WILBERT: "Take it easy, Ray. I hear you telling me you're disappointed you didn't get a larger hamburger. I know you've been saving your money and looking forward to eating here. I'll bring you another burger. While you're waiting, why don't you have that one? Oh, and Ray, they are both on the house—you don't have to pay for them."

RAY RELISH: *(Smiling now.)* "Hey, you know how to keep your customers—and friends like me—happy! Thanks! I'll be coming back here, for sure." *(He starts to eat his hamburger happily.)*

WILBERT: "No problem, buddy."

COREY KETCHUP: "I wonder if Wilbert has had some kind of training in conflict solving? Wait a minute. Wilbert? *(Pauses.)* No, I don't think so! I guess he just got lucky! Hey, Ray, would you like to join me so we don't have to eat our hamburgers alone?"

RAY RELISH: "Sure. Isn't this a great spot?" *(They sit together happily eating their hamburgers.)*

© 1998 by The Center for Applied Research in Education

STICKY SITUATIONS SKIT: "MAD MO"

NARRATOR: "Mo Messy walks into Wilbert's Restaurant. She wants to see what all the excitement is about. Here is a secret: Mo thinks Wilbert is really cool because he opened his own restaurant! Wait until you hear what happens."

WILBERT: *(Sees Mo Messy coming in to sit down.)* "Hi, Mo! Come and sit at the best table in my restaurant. Over here, please. This table faces my kitchen where you can watch me make my awesome hamburgers!" *(Wilbert leads Mo to her table.)*

MO MESSY: "Thanks, Wilbert. Can you bring me one to sample?"

WILBERT: "Sure!" *(Wilbert goes into the kitchen and brings out a hamburger for Mo.)*

MO MESSY: "This looks great, Wilbert. I'm just going to put some mustard on it." *(Mo uses the mustard container and—as she tips it over—it goes all over the place, especially on her clothes.)* "Hey, this mustard just splattered my clothes. My mom is not going to be happy about this! I will get in big trouble! Big Wilbert, how could you have mustard containers with loose tops?" *(Mo is mad.)*

NARRATOR: "Wilbert has to count to himself for a few seconds to calm down. He is mad, too, because he doesn't feel it's his fault the top of the mustard container fell off and got her clothes dirty. After he cools down, he decides how he would feel if he had to go home with mustard stains. Then he looks at the problem differently and decides to solve it so they'll both be happy."

WILBERT: "Mo, let's work this out together. I'll get my special cleaning product. Wilbert's Wonderful Wipe-Out, and try to get the mustard stains out for you."

MO MESSY: "What if that idea doesn't work? How can I leave here and go home with dirty clothes?"

WILBERT: "Let's think of some other possible solutions. If my first idea doesn't work, we could send your clothes to my cleaners, Speedy Sparkly Clean Laundry. They have one-hour service. You could wear one of my cook's jackets while we wait for your clothes."

MO MESSY: "Wilbert, those are good ideas. Let's try to get the mustard out right after I finish this wonderful hamburger."

WILBERT: "OK, Mo. I know we can work this out together. Working out problems is how I got to own this restaurant in the first place! After you finish that hamburger and we get the mustard stains out, let's go make our own sundaes together."

MO MESSY: "That sounds good! Wilbert, you took responsibility for my accident. Not everybody would do that, Wilbert! Let's work on my clothes, then go get those sundaes!"

NARRATOR: "Isn't this a happy ending? Wilbert comes through once again!"

WILBERT'S IN A PICKLE!

SCENE: Wilbert's Restaurant

NARRATOR: "How would you like to visit Wilbert's new restaurant? Picture this scene: the booths you sit at are in the shapes of giant hamburgers. You get your own drinks, whatever you choose, from drink dispensers right at your booth. A table in the middle of the restaurant is shaped like a french fry container that has nothing but french fries on top of it staying warm. You can have free refills! The ketchup squirters are on the sides. For dessert, Wilbert has set up an ice cream stand where you make your own sundaes served with his own whipped cream he invented in all kinds of different flavors! *(Narrator looks up at Anna and Mike.)* Look who's here—Anna and Mike, Wilbert's friends, have just walked into the restaurant."

ANNA: "Hi, Wilbert! How is your brand-new restaurant business?"

WILBERT: "Hi, Anna and Mike! I'm proud of my new restaurant! I'm getting lots of customers coming to try my awesome hamburgers and all the other good stuff. What can I bring my two friends?"

MIKE: "How about giving each of us an awesome burger right now, buddy?"

WILBERT: "No problem, man! Two awesome burgers for my two good friends are coming right up!"

ANNA: "Wilbert, please don't forget the pickles on our burgers."

NARRATOR: "Wilbert was so excited to show off his food to his friends that he tripped carrying a huge jar of pickles. The pickles fell out of the jar with the pickle juice and formed a little stream in the restaurant."

ANNA: "Mike, check out those pickles going past our table!"

MIKE: "Hey, they're heading for that woman who just walked through the door. Yikes!"

WOMAN: *(Enters the restaurant. Stops to talk to Anna and Mike.)* "Well! Well! I've come to see what's all the fuss about these awesome burgers. Now could someone please . . . wo-o-o! Yikes! I'm slipping on something! Help!"

NARRATOR: "The woman slips on a pickle and falls down right into the pickle juice. Her dress gets all sticky and she thinks she might be hurt. Wilbert runs to help her get up and *he* slips and falls down into her lap! He is carrying the two awesome burgers for his friends and one flies into the lady's open mouth. The lady gets very angry and shouts at Wilbert."

WOMAN: "Young man, I might sue your restaurant if my dress is ruined and if I have any broken bones! If I wanted pickles I would have asked for them! Pickles should not greet me when I walk into your restaurant! *You are in a pickle, sonny!*"

WILBERT'S IN A PICKLE! (continued)

NARRATOR: "Wilbert's first reaction is to tell her to take a chill pill! But he knows this restaurant is his responsibility. Wilbert's not sure how to handle the conflict with this angry lady. This was an accident—and she is blaming him. He knows he'd better calm down so he does not say something he'll be sorry for later. He decides to look at this problem *from her point of view,* which is lying on the floor in pickle juice with a hamburger she had not ordered! So Wilbert says to the lady . . ."

WILBERT: "I am so sorry about this mess, uh, madame! Let me help you up. And I won't charge you for the hamburger you just got."

WOMAN: *(Now she's steaming mad.)* "Of course you won't charge me for that hamburger. I didn't order it but it came to me anyway! I came in here to have one of your sundaes with the flavored whipped cream. Now I'm sorry I set my slippery foot into this place!!"

WILBERT: "I'll tell you what I'll do. I will take you over to my ice cream stand and choose whatever you want to order. It will be 'on the house.'"

WOMAN: "What?? You mean that will be spilled, too?"

WILBERT: "No! Ha! Ha! That's just a saying. 'On the house' means I won't give you a bill. You won't have to pay for the sundae or sundaes. Have as many as you want. Will that help to make up for my clumsy accident?"

WOMAN: "Oh, I suppose that would help make up for this mess. And I don't think I broke any bones after all. How many different flavors of whipped cream do you have there, sonny? Show me the way."

MIKE: "Hey, pal, where are our burgers?"

WILBERT: "Mike, can't you see *I'm in a pickle* here?" *(All three friends start to laugh as they look at the floating pickles and pickle juice! Wilbert gets a mop. Mike takes the mop away from him.)*

MIKE: "Let me help you out, Wilbert. I'll mop up this mess for you."

ANNA: "I'll go get the burgers myself so you can get back to what you're best at—making your awesome hamburgers!"

WILBERT: "Cool."

NARRATOR: "The ending to this conflict is a happy one. The woman is so happy with the way Wilbert handled the problem that she decides to come back and bring all her friends. She also gives Wilbert a new recipe for pickles!"

3–58. CELL TALK

Objective:

Children learn to communicate with one another so they all feel like winners while using the TLC steps in a conflict.

Materials Needed:

- "Cell Talk" activity sheet
- Colored posterboard; crayons; markers; scissors; paste

Directions:

1. Review the **TLC steps: T**une in, **L**isten to the other person's side of the conflict, and **C**hoose the best solution so both feel like winners.

2. Pass activity sheets to your students. Tell them they are going to be tuning in to the missing letters in the cell phone message. Give them time to work out the message on the cell phone. Then ask for a volunteer to write on the board the answer: WINNER.

3. Students may then color and cut out their cell phones and paste them on posterboard to give them support. They can do a partner activity solving either a conflict in their lives or one that you give to the whole class. The child holding the cell phone has a turn going through the conflict using the TLC steps to solve it. Then the other partner takes a turn doing the same procedure while holding his or her phone for the same conflict, or a new one of his or her own choosing, or one that you give to the whole class. The role of the partner not holding the phone is to listen and to give feedback as to how the other stayed on track using the TLC steps.

4. Cell phones could either be kept in the students' desks for use with a partner when a conflict arises or hung in the classroom low enough so the children have easy access to them when they want to use them with partners if they are in a conflict.

Bulletin Board Link:

Cell phones create a colorful display with the caption "Talk Out Conflicts Using TLC." If students become involved in a conflict, they can remove their cell phones and, with a partner, go through the TLC steps to solve it.

CELL TALK

Tune in to the conflict-solving message on the cell phone below! *CLUE:* This is how you want both of you to feel after solving your conflict. Now write the message. Then color and cut out your cell phone and glue it to posterboard. Role-play with a partner a conflict you have had or are having now, or make one up.

Using the TLC steps (**T**une in, **L**isten and **C**hoose the best solution) talk on your cell phone to each other and take turns going through the conflict. The next time you're in a conflict with somebody, have an imaginary cell talk!

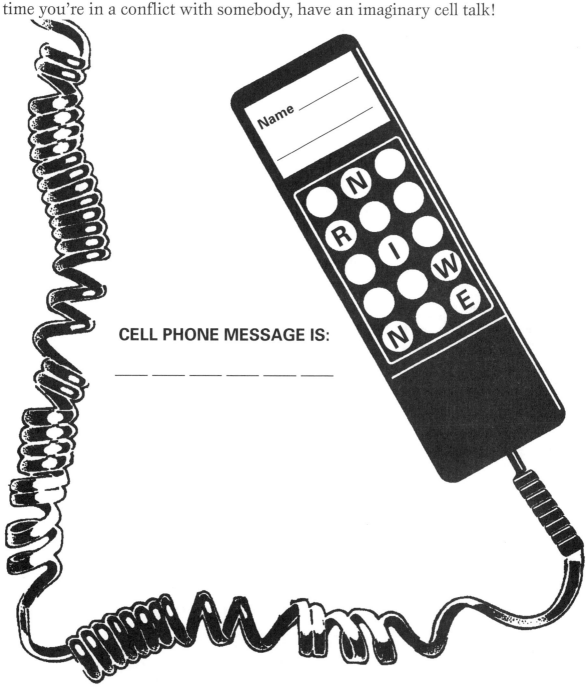

CELL PHONE MESSAGE IS:

___ ___ ___ ___ ___ ___ ___

3–59. "PEACE" TOGETHER PUZZLING CONFLICTS

Objective:

Children give their own peaceful solutions to everyday conflicts they can relate to.

Materials Needed:

- "'Peace' Together Puzzling Conflicts" activity sheet
- Pens; markers; stapler; construction paper; scissors

Directions:

1. Pass the "'Peace' Together Puzzling Conflicts" activity sheets to your class. Tell them they are going to be asked for some peaceful solutions to puzzling conflicts they can relate to. Decide if you are going to read and discuss possible solutions together before the students write them on the sheets or if they will read and complete them individually.

2. Discuss some ideas students have for solving "A Really MESSED-UP Saturday!" *Response:* "Ask your friend to get together next Saturday since you both have plans for this weekend. Make sure you both agree on the exact day. Then make some other plans for this Saturday so you won't be so disappointed."

3. Discuss "Stuck with Peanut Butter." Ask for ideas students have for solving this "sticky" situation. *Response:* "You could tell Jo it was just a mix-up since you had lunch bags that looked alike. Tell Jo you'll be sure to put your name on your bag next time and maybe Jo will do the same. Give Jo's lunch back and ask for your own back. Be glad half of it is still there!"

Role-Plays:

Volunteers rehearse and then role-play the two situations along with their solutions.

"PEACE" TOGETHER PUZZLING CONFLICTS

Write how you would "peace" these puzzles together with a solution everybody feels good about.

A Really MESSED-UP Saturday!

Saturday morning you call your friend all excited to say you are getting a ride over and will stop on the way to rent the video you have both been planning to see. Your friend says she is going to another friend's house and that you had planned to come over Sunday, not Saturday. You're puzzled but you're positive the plan was to go to her house on Saturday! You have plans for Sunday and can't go to her house. You both get really mad. To make peace you . . .

_____

_____

_____

Stuck with Peanut Butter

Your class goes on a field trip and you bring your own lunches. You don't have your name on your plain brown lunch bag and, at lunch time, you find a peanut butter sandwich with no jelly in the bag that isn't yours. Problem is, you hate plain peanut butter! You have an awesome lunch packed in your bag if you could just find it! You look around and see Jo with your lunch. You are both puzzled about who has taken the wrong bag first. And Jo has enjoyed eating half your lunch by now! You start arguing about whose fault it is. To make peace you . . .

_____

_____

_____

3–60. MY OWN CD

Objective:

This is a fun activity to teach children how to describe their conflicts while making CD's.

Materials Needed:

- "My Own CD" activity sheet
- Posterboard; scissors; paste; colored markers; tape; aluminum foil
- *optional:* laminating equipment or clear self-stick vinyl

Directions:

1. Ask your students how many of them enjoy listening to tapes or CD's. (Have a CD to show and play for students who have never seen or heard a CD.) Most of them will probably respond they enjoy CD's. Explain they can now make their own CD's! Pass out activity sheets.

2. There are four steps for this activity in communicating their **C**onflict **D**escriptions or CD's. These steps are on the activity sheet and you may want to write them on the board to discuss:

   1. What was the conflict about?
   2. What did you both want to happen to solve it?
   3. What solution did you both choose?
   4. How did you both feel at the end of the conflict?

3. CD's are traced, cut and pasted onto posterboard that is cut the same size. Students are to choose a conflict they recently had with another person. They write the answers to the four questions about the conflict in the corresponding numbers on the CD. A cover is made by tracing about ³⁄₄ inch less the width of the CD and taping to the CD. Students will enjoy decorating their CD covers. They may choose to design a cover about peace or they can be more specific and make a picture of their recent conflict or solution.

Language Arts Link:

Students write **C**haracter **D**escriptions inside their CD's. They write essays about themselves describing the qualities they have and their favorite things and special people in their lives. An alternative activity is for students to write a CD about another student or special person in their lives.

Music Link:

Children love to make up titles of songs along the theme of peace, such as "Listen to Both Sides Now," "A Matter of Trust," "We Can Work This Out!" Silver foil is cut into a disc to fit inside the cover (may be laminated for a nice effect). Another circle a bit smaller is pasted inside the foil circle (so the foil shows around the circle) with the titles of the songs. The design on the cover of the CD and a title for the CD should carry a theme to complement the selection of songs.

MY OWN

Make your own CD! Write a **C**onflict **D**escription about a conflict you had with another person. In the CD below, tell what happened by answering these questions:

1. What was the conflict about?
2. What did you both want to happen to solve it?
3. What solution did you both choose?
4. How did you both feel at the end of the conflict?

Cut out your CD below and paste it onto sturdy paper. Cut out and decorate a cover (³/₄ inch less the width of the CD) to attach.

1. _____

_____

2. _____

_____

3. _____

_____

4. _____

_____

3–61. PAINT THE BEST APPROACH TO CONFLICT SOLVING

Objective:

Students learn the choices of conflict approaches or styles and the one that achieves a win/win for both involved.

Materials Needed:

- "Paint the Best Approach to Conflict Solving" activity sheet
- Crayons; markers

Directions:

1. Write the five conflict approaches on the board or have them computer-printed and displayed where all your students can read them. The five approaches or styles to conflict are:

   Accommodator: **I give in—You win.**

   Avoider: **I leave—I (sometimes) lose. (Use if conflict is "too hot to handle.")**

   Competitor: **I win—You lose.**

   Compromiser: **You and I give and take, a 50/50 win.**

   Collaborator: **We work together. We both win, 100/100.**

2. Discuss each approach. Point out that the "avoider" approach may not be considered the best win/win approach; however, students must use this approach when tempers are flaring or one of the people in the conflict is physically abusive. If the situation is "too hot to handle," tell students it's OK to walk away from it. Later, after tempers have calmed down, they can confront the conflict.

3. Some students may wonder if the "compromiser" approach is just as good to use as the "collaborator" approach and what the difference is between the two. Explain that with the "compromiser" approach, each person still has to give up something to the other person even though they both win 50/50. With the "collaborator" approach, neither gives up anything. It is a win/win, 100/100 solution. Ask for students to share their own examples of each of the five approaches and how they felt about the way the conflicts ended up. Also ask those students which approach they would choose now.

4. Pass the activity sheets to the students and give students the opportunity to practice the "collaborator" approach. Ask them to think of a conflict and how they will solve it using this approach. On separate paper or the back of the activity sheet, they can "paint a picture" of how both of them will feel at the end of the conflict.

Name _____

PAINT THE BEST APPROACH TO CONFLICT SOLVING

There are five different ways you can approach a conflict. They are:

Accommodator: I give in—You win.

Avoider: I leave—I (sometimes) lose. (Use if conflict is "too hot to handle.")

Competitor: I win—You lose.

Compromiser: You and I give and take, a 50/50 win.

Collaborator: We work together. We both win, 100/100.

Which approach is usually the best? _____ Why?_____

_____

Tell about a conflict you have that you will solve with the "collaborator" approach. Write how you will solve it so you both win.

_____

_____

_____

_____

3-62. I'M OUT OF THIS WORLD SOLVING CONFLICTS SPACE LOG
3-63. STAR POINTS OF MEDIATING
3-64. WE'RE OUT OF THIS WORLD SOLVING CONFLICTS
3-65. PEER MEDIATOR LOG
3-66. MY STELLAR IDEA/ GIVE ME SOME SPACE
3-67. CONFLICT-SOLVER STAR BADGE
3-68. MY AWESOME SPACE TRIP

Objective:

Students keep a log of their conflict-solving efforts to chart their progress with specific conflicts. They also learn the steps of mediation, evaluate how the process works as mediators and participators and, if needed, come up with different ideas for next time. These lessons end with an imaginary space journey on which children choose a gift they would bring back to Earth to help end violence.

Materials Needed:

- "I'm Out of This World Solving Conflicts" cover page; "Star Points of Mediating" sheet; "We're Out of This World Solving Conflicts" activities sheet; "Peer Mediator Log"; "My Stellar Idea," and "Give Me Some Space" activity sheet; "Conflict-Solver Star" badge; "My Awesome Space Trip" teacher sheet
- Stapler; paper clips; spirals to bind conflict-solving logs or hole puncher; colored markers
- Box in Conflict-Solving Center decorated for "My Stellar Idea" sheets

Directions:

1. Pass out "I'm Out of This World Solving Conflicts' Space Log" cover page and activity sheets. Visually display the ten mediation steps from "Star Points of Mediating" using the board, overhead, chart, or large poster made by students on computer. The spaceship theme could be used on the visual display. Encourage the creativity of the students in preparing these displays.

2. Read and discuss the mediation steps together. Ask for volunteers who want to commit to training to be peer mediators. Decide upon a selection process. Also decide on a rotation process so different mediators may mediate. All students who volunteer and *sincerely* want to mediate should have the opportunity to train to become peer mediators. Make clear to students the following points: Any physical conflict or a conflict that in any way threatens to become physically violent should be left to adults to intervene. An adult must be summoned immediately. Peer mediators should not attempt to mediate a physical conflict.

3. Students must attend training sessions that stress all the conflict-solving concepts (found in this book) as background for mediation and, in addition, mediating training. A teacher trained in Peer Mediator Training could meet with students. The first few peer mediations should be done with a teacher sitting in as a silent observer. Once the

teacher feels a student is ready to mediate, students may mediate a problem but always when teachers are available for supervision. A teacher should always be close by during all peer mediations in case tempers flare and the conflict becomes physical.

Note: When a conflict is "too hot to handle" or any indication of physical violence is present, no student should attempt to begin peer mediation. A teacher or other adult should immediately be summoned.

4. Both peer mediators and conflict participants in the mediation process should keep a log for each conflict to evaluate the resolution. Pages for their logs are provided on the activity sheets with questions to be answered after each mediation. The page should be filled out by the two involved in the conflict "We're Out of This World Solving Conflicts" and included in the logs. Mediators fill out the "Peer Mediator Log." If any involved in the mediation are not thoroughly satisfied with how the mediation proceeded, they can make suggestions for what they will do differently next time.

5. Periodically meet with peer mediators and conflict participants in the mediation process to review and discuss their logs. Not all of your students will have conflicts during school time nor will they all be peer mediators. Students who do not get involved in the mediation process either because of the conflicts they have or as mediators should be given time in class to team up with a partner for a conflict each has had recently in their lives. A third student could then play the role of the mediator and the two participants take turns playing out each of their own conflicts. Each partner takes the role of the person with whom the student had the conflict. They then complete the activity sheets in their space logs.

6. The "two-in-one" activity sheet contains two opportunities for students to use either upon completion of their space logs or as the urge arises as they are conflict solving and writing the other sheets for their logs. "My Stellar Idea" gives them the opportunity to express their own ideas for conflict solving in the classroom, on the playground, or in the school. Ideas for home, community, and world issues could also be included for older students. If you have a Conflict-Solving Center, a box needs to be available for these ideas to be dropped in (preferably) anonymously. The box is decorated with stars and is labeled "Our Star (or Stellar) Conflict-Solving Ideas."

    The "Give Me Some Space" activity provides a student who is upset about a conflict to have some quiet time and space to reflect and write about his or her feelings. This may be valuable for the child who is too upset to solve the conflict with the other person and mediation is not working out. It is also helpful if there has been a conflict between yourself or another educator and the child (or someone at home) and he or she acts unusually angry, hurt, or upset. More may be going on with the child than you are aware and writing about how he or she is feeling may help you to better understand the behavior. If *you* fill out how you are feeling about the conflict using the same activity sheet and let the child read *your side* while you read what he or she wrote, you may be able to begin to solve your conflict. A quiet, cooling-down period will enable you both to reflect and to look at the problem from the other's point of view and to realize each other's *feelings* about the conflict.

    "Conflict-Solver Star" badges should be given to each student who attempts to solve a conflict.

7. Take your students on an imaginary space journey. Suggestions for this visualization and the text for the imaginative trip follow at the end of this activity.

Bulletin Board Link:

The "Our Mission Is to Solve Conflicts Peacefully" caption is decorated with a space theme created by students. Display the ten steps of peer mediation. The stars from "My Stellar Ideas" are also displayed.

Music Link:

Play theme music from *2001: A Space Odessey, Star Trek,* or *Star Wars* movies; or the songs "From a Distance" by Bette Midler, "Fly Like an Eagle" by Steve Miller, or "Here Comes the Sun" by George Harrison.

I'M OUT OF THIS WORLD SOOLVING CONFLICTS SPACE LOG

My mission is to go forward to solve conflicts and to help others so that everyone is satisfied with the solution.

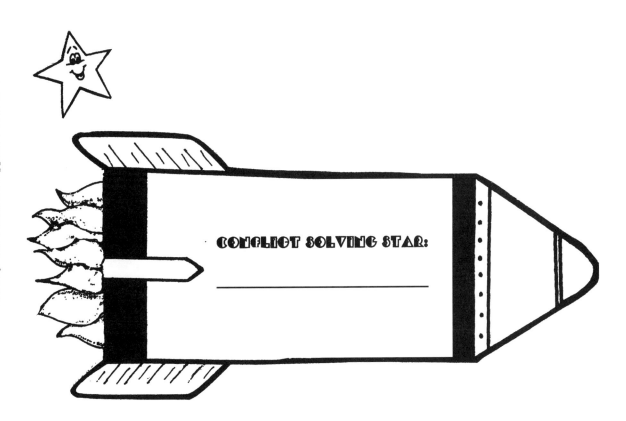

CONFLICT SOLVING STAR:

_____

STAR POINTS OF MEDIATING

Mediators boldly go forward to help others solve conflicts!

© 1998 by The Center for Applied Research in Education

1. Put the two persons in conflict at ease. Explain that they have a choice to be there or not. Ask if they both agree to work on a solution.

2. Tell them all information will be kept confidential among the three of you and you won't judge them.

3. Take turns with each of the two in conflict, tuning in as the other tells his or her point of view.

4. Each one listens as if in the other's shoes and then repeats back the other's words.

5. Ask each person, "What do you want to happen? Why?"

6. Explore and brainstorm solutions so the two in conflict feel like winners.

7. Ask if these possible solutions are fair for both. Which one is the best for both?

8. Choose one solution and ask if they both agree on it. If not, keep trying until both feel like winners.

9. Ask how they both feel. If they agree the solution is good for both, congratulate them (and yourself)!

10. Make a follow-up date to get together to see how well the solution worked and how the two are getting along.

Name _____ Date _____

WE'RE OUT OF THIS WORLD SOLVING CONFLICTS

Our conflict was about _____

_____

Here's how I felt about working it out: _____

_____

Some of the solutions we brain stormed were: _____

_____

The solution we agreed most fair for both of us was _____

_____

Did either of us end up feeling like a loser? _____ Why or why not? ___

_____

How did the mediator help each one of us? _____

_____

Did we plan to get together to follow up? _____ If so, when and where?

_____

Here's how I feel about solving a conflict with a peer mediator: _____

_____

Name _____   Date _____

PEER MEDIATOR LOG

Did both persons having the conflict agree to work on a solution they would both feel good about? Circle **YES** or **NO**. If I answered **NO,** did the mediation end? _____ Explain your answer. _____

_____

_____

The conflict was about _____

_____

_____

Possible solutions were: _____

_____

_____

The solution chosen was: _____

_____

_____

How did each person feel about the solution? _____

_____

_____

Did I *judge* either of them? _____

The hard part for me was _____

_____

_____

Next time I mediate I'll _____

_____

_____

Here's how I feel about this mediation: _____

_____

© 1998 by The Center for Applied Research in Education

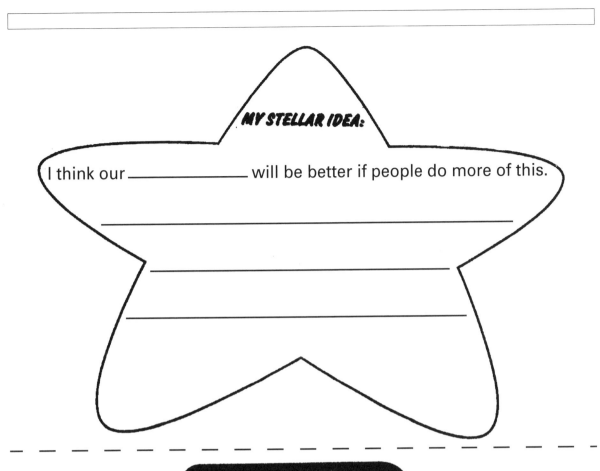

MY STELLAR IDEA:

I think our _____ will be better if people do more of this.

_____

_____

_____

SPACE LOG

Give Me Some Space

Here's what happened in the conflict the way I see It:

_____

Here's how I think _____ sees what happened: _____

_____

Now I feel: _____

I'd like this to happen to make both of us feel better: _____

_____

OUT OF THIS WORLD

STAR:_____

AWESOME CONLICT SOLVER!

MY AWESOME SPACE TRIP

Preparation for Take-Off: Take your students on an imaginary space journey, a visualization, with the purpose of children picturing themselves on a spaceship flying through space, looking down upon Earth and giving our planet a special "secret" that would end violence among people. The suggested text follows below. Choose a time when both you and the children can relax and benefit! A choice of musical selections is offered in the Music Link for "I'm Out of This World Solving Conflicts' Space Log." You may want to also choose a softer classical piece for part of the journey to make it a more relaxing journey.

You are about to have the flight of your life! You are going to fly solo in your own little spaceship you designed yourself. Since you were the creator of your spaceship, picture the details of it, the color, what's inside, your control panel, your space beams control buttons. *(Pause.)* On a real space trip, you'd have to take food that has been dried, but since this is an imaginary trip, you can choose whatever you want to eat. You'll be flying through space for several weeks, so pack lots of your favorite foods! All prepared, you feel ready but a little scared. Off you go! You fly through the cosmos so fast you feel like a time machine. Soon you fly closer to stars and you can't wait to see if they really sparkle up close. *(Pause.)* As you fly closer you discover that, Yes, they *do* twinkle on this imagination journey! You decide to land your spacecraft on one of the sparkling rays that shoots out like a long runway with a landing pad close to the star. You get out and float around the star. You are able to look out and see the Earth so far away.

There are people living happily on the star who look and act differently than people back home on Earth. What do you imagine they look like? *(Pause.)* You try to find out why it's different here and discover it's because all the star people never hurt one another when they get angry. You love living on Earth but you want people to act more like people on this star. You wish and long for a peaceful Earth. If you could bring a *secret* from the star people back to Earth to stop people from hurting each other, what would it be? *(Pause.)* After watching and talking to the loving, peaceful people on the star, you decide what *secret* you will take back to Earth with you. What *secret* would you bring back? *(Pause.)*

As you decide the *secret* you will take back, suddenly the star people sprinkle you with star-dust. *(Pause.)* What does it look and feel like? *(Pause.)* You feel so peaceful inside, now knowing you are going back to Earth to make it a less violent planet. All because you found the *secret* the Earth needs to be peaceful and you know you can spread your knowledge to others. You float back to your spaceship and take off for your flight home. As you get closer to Earth, you don't see sparkles like you just saw on the star, but you know it will shine now, too, if you can spread to others on Earth the secret advice you just learned. They will spread it also and, with lots of dedication to peace, everyone will know about the "gift." You land on Earth and can't wait to share what you saw and learned. And do you know what? You feel like a star! *(Pause.)*

After the visualization:

Continue to play music as children slowly sit up if they have had their heads resting on their desks. Ask them to slowly open their eyes if they were closed. Do not turn all the lights on at once. As a follow-up, ask students to draw what they imagined on their space journeys. Have a circle discussion about the secrets to ending people hurting other people they discovered on their stars. Rely on volunteers rather than calling on children at random as some children may have had difficulty imagining this journey or they may be reluctant to share what they saw in their visualizations.

3–69. TRIANGLES OF TRUST

Objective:

Students practice the role of peer mediator as well as the role of one who has the conflict.

Materials Needed:

- "Triangles of Trust" activity sheet
- Three conflicts given by students and written on board or chart

Directions:

1. Students should review peer-mediation steps from "I'm Out of This World Solving Conflicts Space Log" in their conflict-solving journals before beginning this activity.

2. Ask for recent conflicts students in your class have experienced. Choose three to write on the board. Only write the summary of what the conflict was about—not the solution.

3. Divide your class into groups of three. Each member of the group takes a turn in the role of the person with the conflict as well as the role of mediator. Groups use the three different conflicts given by the class and written on the board for all groups to read. Remind students that for this activity to be effective, they need *to act like they are really having the conflict they are role playing* and to pretend they are seeking the best solution. When the student takes the role of *peer mediator,* he or she *writes the answers to the questions on the activity sheet.* Enabling students to experience the role of peer mediator is a valuable conflict-solving tool whether or not they go on to be peer mediators.

4. After students leave their groups of three, have a class discussion with questions to find out their feelings about taking the role of a peer mediator. Ask: "Would you like to be a peer mediator? Why? Why not?" *Responses:* "I didn't like the responsibility of being a peer mediator." "I found it too hard not to offer my own solutions instead of letting the two having the conflict decide the best way to solve it." "I felt so helpful that I want to become a peer mediator." "I liked leading them to the very best solution so they both ended up feeling like they had won. I felt good!"

TRIANGLES OF TRUST

 Write the answers to the questions below *when it is your turn to be the peer mediator.*

1. Take turns telling what happened from each of your points of view. *"Here's how I saw it . . ."*

 Name_____

Name_____

2. Put yourself in the other's shoes. Listen and repeat the words back. *"I hear you saying . . ."*

 3. What do you each want to happen to solve this problem? Take turns saying your interests.

Name_____

 Name_____

4. What are some *fair* ideas to brainstorm so you *both* end up happy with the solution?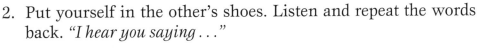

5. Which of these ideas will be the *best* solution for each one of you so you both feel happy?

Name_____

Name_____

6. The solution agreed on is: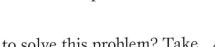

7. How do you both feel with our solution? Is it a solution so everyone feels like a winner?

Name_____

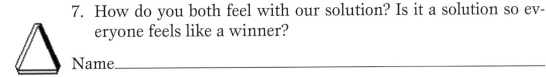

Name_____

3–70. LET'S PARTY!

Objective:

Children review many of the concepts found in this book's activities.

Materials Needed:

- "Let's Party!" activity sheet
- Colored markers; crayons; pencils

Directions:

1. Pass out the crossword puzzle activity sheets to your class. They will see the familiar comic figure, Wilbert, now all excited about his birthday party. As noted on the top of their activity sheets, Wilbert isn't sure who to invite so he decides to invite the kids who have the qualities listed on the crossword puzzle. (Those qualities are all the concepts the students have learned about in previous activities.) *Answer to party message:* Kids have *good times* at parties! Answers to crosswod puzzle:

2. Decide if you are going to duplicate the puzzle on the board and do it together as a class, or if you prefer to have students form small groups to work on the puzzle together, or to have them complete the puzzles individually.

3. Your students may enjoy combining this crossword puzzle with another "party" theme activity, such as "Balloosters" or "My Loot Bag of Goodies" from Section 2. Have students form small groups and pass their sheets to each child in the group who then writes something positive about them. You can have some party decorations to make the activities more festive. If you have a "skills for life" period in your classroom each week, the children will look forward to this day.

4. Because this activity is intended to be a review of concepts children have learned in previous activities in this book, plan this as an activity after you have completed all the concepts included in the crossword puzzle.

Bulletin Board Link:

Make a large version of the crossword puzzle on the bulletin board. If you want to display Wilbert, enlarge the picture of Wilbert, who could be emerging from the crossword puzzle. Decorate the background with some inexpensive party supplies such as horns, blowers, and streamers. Completed copies of the "My Loot Bag of Goodies" activity make colorful displays. Balloons made from colorful paper with each child's name and hung by ribbons together with others from their cooperative groups also add to the festive theme. The caption is "Please Come to Wilbert's Party!" or "Our Party Time!"

Party Guest _____ Date _____

LET'S PARTY!! CROSSWORD PUZZLE

Wilbert is having a party! But he's having trouble knowing who to invite. He decides to invite kids he really likes to be around. He made a list of the things he likes about other kids. See if you can find his favorite things about others on the crossword below. By the way, YOU are invited!

Across:

Wilbert likes kids who usually do these things:

1. Do this when they're very angry. They _____ down first.
2. Turn their dreams into _____ and set a date to achieve them.
3. Take _____ saying what they both want when solving a conflict.
4. Know their _____ go up and down every day.

Down:

5. _____ to the other person's point of view.
6. Know that to have friends, you need to be a _____ to others.
7. Need to know some positive things about his or her own _____.
8. Act _____ to others when they are put down.

Choose from these words:

self   calm   turns   kind   friend   good   feelings   times   listen   goals

Fill in this party message from the *two words* that did *not* fit into the puzzle:
Kids have _____ _____ at parties!

3-71. MY PEACE RIPPLERS BOOK
3-72. PEACE RIPPLERS

Objective:

Children realize that each *small act* of kindness causes a ripple effect that starts out small and spreads quite far to create peace in our world.

Materials Needed:

- "My Peace Ripplers Book" cover page
- "Peace Ripplers" activity sheet
- *Optional:* blue background paper; blue markers; crayons
- Paper for additional pages for a peace rippler booklet

Directions:

1. Discuss the meaning of the term "ripple." *Responses:* "A ruffle on the surface of water." "A ripple is what you make when you throw a stone into calm water. It ripples or spreads to make more ripples." Ask what they think the word "rippler" means. *Response:* "A rippler is somebody who makes the first ripple and then the ripples spread."

2. Write the following quotation on the board and have students computer-print a large copy to hang in your classroom:

   "No one could make a greater mistake than he who did nothing because he could only do a little." —Edmund Burke

   Discuss together the meaning of this quotation. *Response:* "Sometimes we don't do anything because we don't think it's enough and wonder if we should bother at all. We should remember every little bit helps." Students write their own meanings on their activity sheets. Ask students for examples of how a little bit can help a cause. *Responses:* "If we collect money for victims of a disaster and if everyone gives even a small amount, it will all add up to help." "I help out by picking up and throwing away lunch bags and trash I find on the playground."

3. Ask children for examples of things they can do to help create a ripple effect toward getting rid of violence and creating a peaceful world. *Responses:* "You can start in your own family and school by doing helpful things for others." "You can start to understand differences in other people whether it's the way they act, dress, or the color of their skin." "Get to know people on the inside." After the discussion, make the point that each small act of understanding and kindness to others chips away at violence.

4. Students create their own ideas for "Peace Rippler" stories or poems after reading the poem on the bottom of the activity sheet (which is used as a cover). Additional pages are filled with their own ideas for peace ripplers. These can be ideas to use within your classroom and extending to the whole school and the community depending on the students' ages. Ideas for more peaceful playgrounds have been used in schools with designated students as the "peace ripplers" at recesses. They may initiate noncompetitive games if they include all students who want to play.

Bulletin Board Link:

After children have written their own poems or stories, display them for the rest of the school. Your class is starting the ripple effect and others will be encouraged to follow. If the whole school decides to continue the peace rippler effect, they could also write about peace ripplers on an oceanic background in your front hall. Each student's ripple idea is written on an ocean wave. Display the waves drowning the words printed or pictures depicting the following terms: "violence," "racism," "cultural differences," "prejudice," "wars," and "hatred."

MY *PEACE RIPPLERS* BOOK

WE'RE THE PEACE RIPPLERS

We're the Peace Ripplers
here to create a nonviolent world.
Our acts of kindness will spread
like ripples that chip away at violence.

Little ripples start out small
and spread one after the other
until HUGE waves are formed
to wash away racism and wars.

Our ocean of kindness will then be calm
and the ripples can relax and smile
as violence is drowned and peace comes
to all who were touched by its waves.

Name _____

Name _____

PEACE RIPPLERS

"No one could make a greater mistake than he who did nothing because he could only do a little."

—EDMUND BURKE

Write what this quotation means to you.

_____

_____

_____

_____

If you throw a stone into still water, do you have fun watching the ripples spread to make more ripples? It is called a *ripple effect.* You can start a ripple effect of peace with kind acts to others. Below write kind acts you will do for two others.

PERSON	KIND ACT
1. _____	_____
_____	_____
2. _____	_____
_____	_____

4
Conflict-Resolution Activities for Your School

"A teacher is not someone who stands at the front of the room and imparts information that he or she thinks is important. A teacher is someone who is working with kids in groups and is taking the information and their lives into account. That teacher loves kids unconditionally, because every single child has goodness, every child has sparks, and no child is bad. As soon as my relationship opens up with a child, I can do my job to prepare kids to become successful in meeting the challenges of the 21st century."

Karen Grose, Grade 6 teacher

4–1. TEACHERS' "BULLY BUSTERS!"

What Is Bullying?

Bullying is repeated emotional or physical abuse involving an imbalance of power between a bully and a targeted victim.

How Can You Spot a Bully?

- A bully usually has low self-esteem. Putting others down physically or emotionally is one way the bully has of building up self.
- A bully has often been a victim of bullying. After being picked on, he or she picks on others.
- A bully wants to win regardless of the "cost" of the win.
- A bully is often unpopular and seeks to gain attention, even if it's negative.
- A bully has a strong need to dominate. "I should get what I want no matter how I do it."
- A bully often has confidence in his or her own physical strength.
- A bully lacks empathy for victims.
- A bully feels little or no guilt for abusive actions, convinced they are deserved by the victim.
- A bully is aggressive and lacks assertion skills.

What Does a Bully Do?

A bully chooses a victim so there is an imbalance of power between the bully and the victim in emotional or physical strength. Bullying involves repeated negative actions against the victim.

Emotional abuse of victim may include: intimidating, name-calling, threatening, teasing, taunting, making fun of family, writing graffiti (ethnic), alienating socially

Physical abuse of victim may include: punching, slapping, tearing clothes, shoving, spitting, threatening with or using a weapon, stealing

What Can You Do to Help a Bully?

Build up a bully's self-esteem by:

- Make bully aware of his or her positive qualities; do "positive identity" activities.
- A bully needs to feel a sense of belonging and security in your classroom.
- Do goal-setting activities with the bully; give him or her positive direction to direct his or her goals.
- Friendship-building exercises will teach the bully how to make friends in positive ways rather than seeking attention in negative ways.

Give the bully classroom positions of positive power as:

- Music DJ, Library Linker, Conflict Corner Organizer, Bulletin Board or Around-the-School Artiste, Mentor to other students in an area he or she enjoys, Pet Caretaker, Attendance Deliverer, etc.
- Do *empathy role-plays* with the bully to develop compassion for the victim. First, role-play a scene where the victim is hurt. Next, role-play showing the hurt that the victim feels and then children helping the victim feel better.

How Can You Spot a Victim of a Bully?

- A victim is chosen for an imbalance of power—either physically or emotionally.
- A victim is often passive when bullied.
- A victim does not have the need to dominate.
- A victim may be physical or emotionally weaker than the bully.
- A victim is usually nonviolent.
- A victim lacks assertion skills.
- A victim may be popular who the bully tries to humiliate.
- A victim is usually nonaggressive.
- A victim finds it difficult to defuse the bully.

What Can You Do to Help a Victim?

- Teach the victim how to be *assertive.*
- Make the victim realize he or she is not helpless or defenseless against the bully.
- Reassure the victim you will provide protection from the bully in your classroom.
- Teach the victim how to defuse the bully by being firm and direct or by using humor.
- Share responsibility by asking, "How could you act differently so bullying won't continue?" *Responses:* "I will look the bully right in the eye and say I won't let the bully put me down." "I'll tell the bully I will get help if he or she hurts me in any way and I'll mean it!" "I must remember that nobody can make me feel low unless I allow them to."
- Assign a buddy system when out of the classroom.
- Hold regular class meetings.

What Role Do the Bystanders Play in Bullying?

- Approach anti-bullying at both the classroom and the whole school levels. Bystanders must know the crucial role they play; without others watching them bully, a bully does not have the audience he or she seeks.
- Provide empathy awareness through role playing in which children play out and then hold a class discussion about the hurt the victim of bullying feels.
- Teach children that to passively watch a child being bullied is to be guilty of bullying by providing the bully with the attention needed, sought, and fulfilled.

- Give students alternatives to passively watching the bullying episode: they should not stand and watch but should instead disband the "spectator group," get help from the nearest teacher and urge others to come along so it is a group rather than one child asking for help. If they cannot persuade others to join them, a child should be encouraged to go for help alone.

Who Should Be Involved in Dealing with Bullies, Victims, and Bystanders?

The entire school community should be involved in a "Bully Busters!" program. Bullying creates fear not only within the victims of bullying but in the general atmosphere of the school because the other students become fearful also. *All educators, parents, and students* must be made aware of the intertwining roles the bully, the victim, and the bystander all play to make the bullying incident a "success" in the eyes of the bully and a heartbreaking experience for the victim.

- The School Behavior Code should include "Bully Busters!" to discourage bullying attempts.

- Hold a parent "Bully Busters!" session to inform all parents of signs to watch for in their children playing any of the three roles in a bullying situation. Make it a "We'll all work together!" process to solve this problem.

- Individual parent meetings may be needed to address the bully's or the victim's needs. These meetings should be a non-intimidating, non-blaming session for the parents who may feel reluctant to attend, or perhaps guilty for their roles in the formation of the qualities of the bully and the victim. Stress that your intent is *not to look for blame* but *to go forward with them* to help their children!

- Class meetings create the opportunity to air out anti-bullying suggestions from the whole class and lend a "We're all in this together!" atmosphere in the classroom. Responsibility is given to the students themselves to come up with *ideas of their own* to stop bullying. These class meetings also help to air out resentment and negative feelings.

- Hold periodic "chill-out" times with each of your students. Indications of bullying by bullies themselves, bystanders, or victims may come up in your informal talks. (Refer to the Chill-Out Chart in this book.) *You cannot help them if you don't know about the incidents* and often children keep the acts hidden; however, the memories may never be forgotten. Make the time for these meetings between just the two of you!

4–2. BULLY BUSTERS! POSTER
4–3. WHY DO KIDS BULLY?
4–4. ARE YOU A BULLY BUSTER?

Objective:

Children learn how the three roles involved in the bullying process—the bully, the victim and the bully watchers (or bystanders) enable bullying acts.

Materials Needed:

- "BULLY BUSTERS!" poster, "Why Do Kids Bully?" "Are You a Bully Buster?"
- Markers; crayons; paper for poster contest

Directions:

1. Pass out "BULLY BUSTERS!" posters containing six anti-bullying points to your class. Enlarge the page to poster size to display in your classroom. Divide students into small groups to discuss the points on the poster and to ask questions. After the groups have completed their discussions, hold a class discussion on points and questions that came up in small groups. Don't rush this session as you wait for children's concerns to emerge.

   For example, children may not realize that reporting a bullying incident is not tattling. Children may fear reporting an incident for fear the bully may come after them. Encourage groups of children to stick together and get help from an adult if a bullying incident occurs. Explain that is why you want to make anti-bullying a classroom and, if possible, a whole school effort after gaining the support of the entire school to discourage bullying.

2. The "Why Do Kids Bully?" activity sheets, and the "Are You a "Bully Buster?" surveys are passed to your students to complete individually after you have introduced them and fully discussed the poster steps.

3. Children should be encouraged to express an experience they have had either as a victim of a bully or as a bully to others. After they finish their activity sheets, ask volunteers to discuss their personal experiences. Choose volunteers to share any of the answers on their activity sheets. Avoid calling on any child who is reluctant to relate an experience about either being a victim or about bullying other children. Have a private time with any of these children.

4. Have a "BULLY BUSTERS!" poster contest. Display posters all around the school. If bullies see lots of anti-bullying information surrounding them, they may re-think bullying as a way to get others' attention. The posters will also make bully victims and bully watchers aware of taking responsibility for their roles in the bullying process.

Bulletin Board Link:

Have students draw a large fence to display in the classroom above the boards or make a bulletin board display with a winding fence long enough so that children can make small replicas of themselves (class pictures could be used with children attaching their bodies). Each student's replica has a quotation (above or below) of his or her own best idea for discouraging bullying in your school.

BULLY BUSTERS!

NEWS "BULLY-TIN"

Bullies can't bully without any *victims* or anybody *to watch* them bully!

1. Ask an adult for help immediately if you are ever physically hurt or if you see anyone being hurt.

2. If you are often made fun of or have your family made fun of, or if you are hurt in any way, you have been a bully victim. Get help from an adult.

3. Don't blame yourself if a bully keeps putting you down. The bully has a problem; *not you.* Your problem is only if you *allow* a bully to put you down.

4. Be firm when you are victimized or put down by making eye contact with the bully and saying, "I won't take your abuse."

5. Understand the bully is trying to have power over you. You need to show the bully that you will not be controlled. Say, "You can't control me!"

6. Let the bully know you won't stand around and watch bullying happen to somebody else. You will not be a bully watcher. Get help as a group from adults.

7. Most of all, make the bully realize *you* are NOT a good choice for a victim!

WHY DO KIDS BULLY?

Have you ever been pushed around or threatened or teased? If it happened several times by the same person, you may have been the victim of a *bully*. Write below about a time you were bullied and tell what you did and how you felt about the bully.

_____
_____
_____
_____
_____
_____

Read the ***Bully Busters!*** poster. Write how you would handle a bullying situation now that you know what to do. If you have bullied somebody else, write what you would do next time you feel like being a bully.

_____
_____
_____
_____
_____
_____

ARE YOU A "BULLY BUSTER"?

These questions and answers will help your school with bullies, their victims, and bully watchers. It is your choice to sign your name on this sheet. If you are in danger of being hurt, let an adult know right away. Look at the dark words and circle your answers.

1. I think I am a **bully; victim; bully watcher; none of these.**

2. I feel **safe** or **scared** by other(s) in my classroom. If scared, explain why.
    _____
    _____

3. I feel **safe** or **scared** on the playground at recesses. If scared, explain why.
    _____

4. I feel **safe** or **scared** coming to and going home from school. If scared, explain why: _____
    _____

5. Somebody has hurt me more than twice since school began this year: **YES** or **NO.** If yes, explain what happened. _____
    _____

6. Do you feel you can ask for and get help *if you are bullied?* **YES** or **NO.** Explain your answer. _____
    _____
    _____

8. Where would you get help if you *saw someone else being bullied?* Explain your answer. _____
    _____
    _____

9. Have you hurt someone since the start of school? **YES** or **NO.** Explain your answer. _____
    _____
    _____

10. On the back of this page write a good "bully buster" idea *you* have to help get rid of bullying.

4–5. BARRELS OF BULLY BUSTERS

Objective:

Primary children are introduced to the term "bully" and learn how to discourage bullying.

Materials Needed:

- "Barrels of Bully Busters" activity sheet
- Scissors; colored markers; crayons

Directions:

1. Write the word "bully" on the board. Have a circle time with your students to discuss what this word means to them. *Responses:* "A bully is mean to other kids." "Bullies pick on kids who are smaller." Write "Bully Busters" and "discourage" on the board. Explain that this lesson will teach them *Bully Busters* or ways to make bullies feel like giving up on their intended victims.

2. Ask children why they think some children bully others. *Response:* "A bully is mean to other kids because somebody was mean to her or him." Most will not be able to answer this question and that is the reason for it. It is important from an early age that children learn about *bullying,* why kids bully other kids. The primary level is not too soon to teach them. You need to make these points: A bully seeks control or power over the victim chosen. Often a bully has been a victim of bullying. A bully often chooses a weaker or smaller child as his or her victim.

3. Explain to young children that there are a number of steps they can take if they find themselves as victims of bullying or are in the position of watching someone else being bullied. We can call these Bully Busters! Say that if a young child refuses to be victimized either by making it known in a manner firm and direct enough that a bully knows the intended victim means business or by seeking adult help (especially in the case of physical harm), a bully will be discouraged. Tell your class if they all resist being the victim of bullying, the bully will find it difficult to find a child to bully. If they realize the role they play simply by standing by and watching, there will be fewer silent witnesses to bullying. With these awarenesses come two of the detriments a bully needs: no victim and no audience!

4. When students return to their desks after you have completed your circle discussion, pass out activity sheets. Inside their barrels, students write the letters of the good ideas they choose to discourage bullies. Their letters spell a word they are to write at the bottom of the barrels. *The clue:* If everyone in our class and in our school uses these ideas to discourage bullies, we can say this to the bullies. **The word is: goodbye.**

Bulletin Board Link:

The caption is "We Have Barrels of Ideas for Bullying." Display students' barrels that they cut out with their ideas to discourage bullying.

Name _____

BARRELS OF BULLY BUSTERS

Wilbert has fallen into a barrel of Bully Busters! These are ideas so bullies won't bully anymore. In your barrel below, write the letters of good ideas to discourage bullies. At the bottom of the page, write the word your letters spell. **Clue:** We can say this to bullies if we all use Bully Busters!

D. Let a bully help out with you in the classroom.

A. Act afraid of the bully and cry.

G. Understand the bully needs to feel control over someone weaker or smaller.

P. Let the bully control you.

O. Don't stand by and watch anyone bully.

Y. Get help if you or somebody else is in physical danger.

O. Tell bullies you will *not* be a victim of their bullying.

E. Make direct eye contact with a bully even if you are smaller.

B. Understand the bully has often been bullied.

We'll say this to bullies with our barrels of Bully Busters!

— — — — — — —

4–6. A CONFLICT-RESOLUTION CELEBRATION

Why not hold a meaningful, fun celebration of conflict-resolution activities—a day or part of a day devoted to handling anger, bullying, and awareness of alternatives to violence? You may want to culminate the day with an all-school assembly in which classes perform skits and lead the assembly in selected songs. Suggestions are given below for planning a Conflict-Resolution Celebration.

1. If you decide to make your celebration schoolwide, enlist a planning committee of supportive teachers, principal or vice principal, along with students. An alternative is to have classes do their celebrations on separate dates. The class could choose to hold an assembly and invite the rest of the school. Other classes hold their celebrations on separate dates. If this approach is chosen, it is important to keep in mind that the aim of the celebration activities is for both you and the children to *enjoy* participating while they learn skills in conflict solving. Competitions among classes with elaborate displays and performances are *not* the objective.

2. Participating educators choose conflict-solving activities to do with their groups and name the activities on the included sign-up sheet. A list of classroom activity suggestions is provided later in this section or they may prefer to choose activities of their own.

3. Each class meets for 20 minutes, then rotates. If the entire school is participating, the bell could ring every 20 minutes so that everyone is on schedule to rotate. If only a certain number of classes is participating, appointed student helpers could remind each class to rotate. Students are then to be instructed as to the locations of their next classroom activities. There are five-minute intervals for rotating. Student helpers guide younger students to their next activities as well as assist with the preparation for the activities.

4. Decide whether or not to hold an all-school assembly, either as a way of starting off the day or as a culmination activity at the close. If there is to be an assembly, decide which classes will be participating and what each will contribute. If the entire school has chosen a song or songs to be performed at the assembly, it is a good idea to have the tapes played or sung over the intercom several days so that all the students can learn the words (at least to the refrains) and sing along. Someone may have a wonderful idea for an inspiring song or you may use the songs suggested in this book.

5. Name tags for each student may be written on the doves in this book as symbols of peace. Name tags will enable teachers to learn names of students in the school other than those in their own classrooms. The dove forms can also be used for students to write peace poems. The peace doves may be hung in the front hall, welcoming all to your Conflict-Resolution Celebration!

4–7. FUN IDEAS FOR YOUR CONFLICT-RESOLUTION CELEBRATION

Choose one of the ideas below (or create your own) to be *your* celebration activity.
(**Note:** These activities correlate to sheets given in earlier sections of the book.) If you do not use your classroom, choose another area in the school that may be better suited for your activity. Student helpers can help with your preparation and also with rotation if the whole school celebrates together. Complete the sign-up sheet so that activities aren't repeated. Have fun with your groups!

1. **Nacho Time!** Divide children into groups of six. Pass out sombreros (student helpers may prepare paper sombreros) to each child with slits in the center. Children cut out five paper "nachos" and put their names at the top of each one. They pass their nachos to the left to each group member to write one positive quality about the child. The child receives five nachos to place in his or her sombrero. Sombreros may then be decorated. Serve a Mexican treat. Olé!

2. **Tickled Pink!** *(for primary students)* Have your area done in pink—paper tablecloths for large tables with pink sparkles scattered in the center, pink lights or candles if closely monitored, napkins, and a pink snack such as pink lemonade in pink paper cups or pink grapefruit sections. Pass activity sheets from Section 2 as you explain that the title means we are very excited about something. Have a group discussion giving examples of our successes. Ask them to write what it is *about themselves* that tickles them pink. *Example:* A recent success they have had or a kind act they have done.

3. **We're Sparkling Gems.** For this activity, use the "Diamonds" activity sheet from Section 1. Divide students into groups of six to pass their sheets to each member of the group to sign a shining quality about each child in the group. Make sure no child passes on writing a positive comment on the sheets. Have shiny foil to use as background paper for students to cut out and mount their diamonds. Decorate the area with anything that sparkles.

4. **Snowflakes.** Discuss cooperation with your group and the importance of each child's unique contributions. Provide different pastel-colored papers for students to cut out and write their unique qualities in their snowflakes. Display these in the hall with the caption "Each One of Us Is Unique! Just Look at What We Can Do When We Stick Together."

5. **Put Yourself in Somebody Else's Shoes.** Play a game of "I Want What You Have" with each partner trying to convince the other to give up his or her "gift" without offer of money or force. (You may use real objects or pictures of objects kids would like.) Students see what a problem is like from another's viewpoint—the other person's shoes—when they reverse the roles.

6. **What Makes You Pop?** Cut pale yellow or white paper into large popcorn kernels. Inside the kernels children write essays or draw pictures about the qualities they have that "make them pop." Be sure to consider having fresh air-popped popcorn available in large bowls. Primary children enjoy standing behind a large popcorn container (made by your student helpers) and "popping up" with their kernels.

7. **A Peaceful Time!** *(for relaxation)* Soft music is played while children are taken on an imagination journey in which they picture a peaceful situation. You may use the visualization presented earlier in this book or make up your own journey for the children.

8. **Precious Petals.** Offer an art activity whereby the children make paper flowers. They then fill in the qualities needed to attract friends in the petals. (See "Precious Petals.")

9. **Tasty Toppings.** Student helpers make pizzas, hamburgers, hot dogs, enchiladas, or sundaes out of posterboard or construction paper. They then make toppings for the items. Students write positive qualities about themselves inside each topping and paste onto the items. If you display them, the caption could be "Our Deluxe Qualities!"

10. **Mad Hatters' Tea Party.** Play the listening game from "Twisted Tales." Divide primary students into small groups and older students into larger groups. Have various categories (pizza toppings, school subjects, ice cream flavors, etc.) on cards prepared for groups to draw from a variety of hats (real or made of paper with slits for the cards). The children repeat the category to the next person in the group. Serve a simple snack on a lovely table.

11. **Jumpin' Jellybeans!** Colorful paper is cut into large jellybeans. Everyday conflict situations are provided by the students and written on the board. One is chosen to be worked out by students individually on their jellybeans as they write their conflict-solving plan. Primary students may dictate or draw pictures on their jellybeans.

12. **Easel Conflict Solving.** Colorful paper is cut into large paintbrushes, palettes, and paint blobs for students to write about how they would solve a real-life conflict (use real-life scenarios written on cards and read aloud for students to solve). Students are asked to use the three steps of the TLC Recipe from this book. Display finished essays in the hall with the caption "Color Us Unique at Solving Conflicts" on posterboard.

13. **Pasta Party.** Children realize after a class discussion about our different preferences for pasta that not everyone has the same reaction to the same event. Distribute the "Spaghetti, Spaghetti!" activity sheets from Section 3. Go Italian for this activity with checkered tablecloths and offer breadsticks or cookies and have a display table with as many sample dry pastas as possible.

14. **TLC Poster Contest.** TLC posters from this book are passed out to students to color and to display around the school. On the back of the posters, students are challenged to design their own posters using the TLC (Tender Loving Care) approach. Or they can make up a new approach to conflict-solving and design a poster using the new approach. (Hold a contest and send the winning poster to me, Beth Teolis, at 149 Coldstream Avenue, Toronto Ontario, M5N 1X7, for possible future publication and a congratulatory letter!)

15. **Line Up Against V-I-O-L-E-N-C-E.** Each student receives one letter of the word "violence" and writes a word contributing to violence that begins with that letter. The student then writes a short essay about how he or she feels the word chosen contributes to violence. *Example:* **V**engeance. The child writes how vengeance contributes to violence. Choose the most expressive words and articles for each letter. They are then recited by their authors at your conflict-resolution activities assembly. Each child holds up a posterboard with his or her letter, forming a line to spell the word "violence."

16. **What's My Style?** Cut out five paper hats, ties, or large "C's" with the five conflict styles (refer to the "Paint the Best Approach to Conflict Solving" activity sheet in this book) and descriptions on each. Pass one to each of five students. Given a real-life conflict - such as a conflict over a loaned video game not returned - the students act out their given conflict styles in a role-play with a partner.

17. **We're Hot Stuff Solving Conflicts!** Ahead of time, enlarge and cut out the chili pepper from "We're Hot Stuff!" Paste the enlarged chili pepper onto red posterboard, add a small circle at the top for yarn to go through for hanging, and duplicate it for the number of children who will be doing this activity. Students write on each pepper a plan they will use to "cool down" when they're angry. *Examples:* "Calm down before I begin to solve the conflict." "Tune in to the other person, not just to my own needs." "Listen to the other person's side of the problem. Each child receives a piece of green yarn to hang his or her pepper. Display the peppers together hanging from twine rope in your classroom.

18. **We're Out of This World (Handling Our Anger).** (for primary students) Cut out colorful spaceships for each child to draw, write, or dictate how he or she should first "cool off" when angry as an alternative to "taking off" when angry by hitting or shouting. An alternative art activity could be offered using plasticine. Children work alone or in pairs to make spaceships showing themselves in the astronauts' places. Spaceships may be displayed on a table in the hall.

19. **Much Music!** This area will offer a variety of music for the children to enjoy. Choose your selections from those suggested in this book or your own choices you feel appropriate. An especially "classroom-enjoyed" song is "Life Is a Highway" by Tom Cochrane. Students enjoy singing along and younger students may pretend to be driving. Group discussion could precede the song to point out that students could go along their own highways of life being driven by peer pressure and the values of others, or they could decide their own values and be their own drivers on their highways of life.

20. **It's Party Time!** Divide children into groups of six. Use the "BALLOOSTERS" activity sheet. Each child in the group writes a positive quality about the child whose name is at the top of the activity sheet. Then the activity sheet "A Loot Bag of Goodies" could be used for students to decorate and fill out special qualities about their favorite people. A room festooned with colorful balloons, music, and a party atmosphere will attract the children.

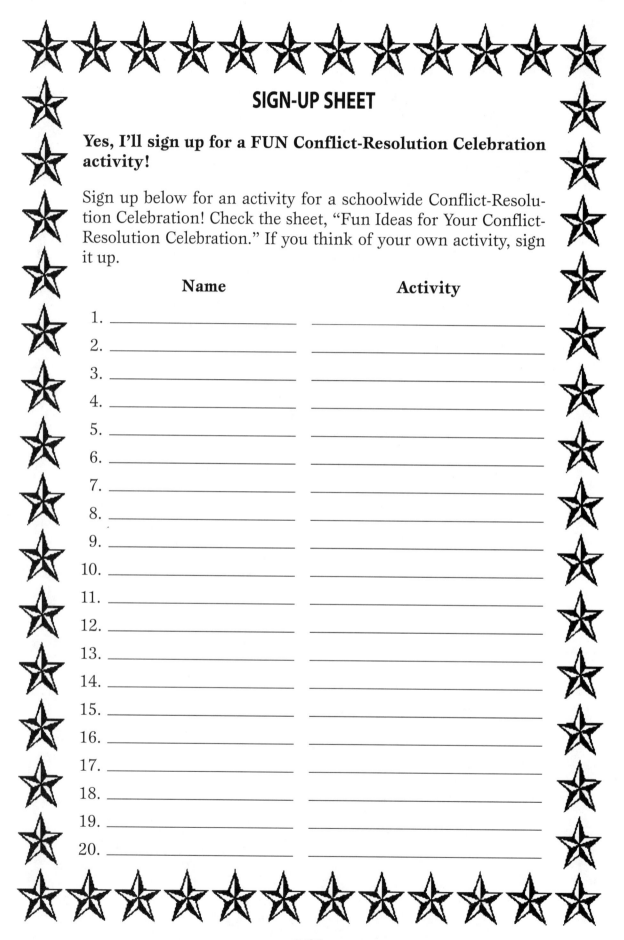

SIGN-UP SHEET

Yes, I'll sign up for a FUN Conflict-Resolution Celebration activity!

Sign up below for an activity for a schoolwide Conflict-Resolution Celebration! Check the sheet, "Fun Ideas for Your Conflict-Resolution Celebration." If you think of your own activity, sign it up.

Name	Activity
1.	
2.	
3.	
4.	
5.	
6.	
7.	
8.	
9.	
10.	
11.	
12.	
13.	
14.	
15.	
16.	
17.	
18.	
19.	
20.	

4–8. MUSIC FOR YOUR CONFLICT-RESOLUTION CELEBRATION

Enjoy music while learning peace and conflict solving from the lyrics of one of the songs below or of your own or the students' choices. If you aren't musically gifted, borrow a recording of the song, play it for the group, and soon they will be singing along! Words to the song should be visually available on paper and/or chart or board. (Your student helpers could help to prepare a copy of the words to the song ahead of time.) If an assembly is planned, you may choose to teach each of your classes one of the songs to be performed by a class at the assembly so that all classes can join in singing together. Sign up your chosen song on the Conflict-Resolution Celebration "Sign-Up Sheet" or join together with another class (or more) to perform a song at the assembly. Below is a list of songs. You may also enjoy singing some of these songs at graduation

- "A Smile Like Yours" by Natalie Cole*
- "Colors Of The Wind"by Vanessa Williams*
- "Change The World" by Eric Clapton*
- "Go The Distance" by Michael Bolton*
- "Power Of The Dream" by Celine Dion*
- "What A Wonderful World" by Louis Armstrong*
- "Angels Among Us" by Alabama*
- "Can You Feel The Love Tonight?" by Elton John*
- "Circle Of Life" by Elton John*
- "Hero" by Mariah Carey*
- "Lean on Me" by Bill Withers*
- "One Moment in Time" by Whitney Houston*
- "The Rose" by Bette Midler*
- "The Living Years" by Mike and The Mechanics*
- "The Dance" by Garth Brooks*

- "Yes, I Can" by Baldy*
- "Between Friends" by Richard Samuels*
- "Count on Me" by Whitney Houston
- "Forever Yesterday, For The Children" by Gladys Knight
- "From a Distance" by Bette Midler
- "He Ain't Heavy; He's My Brother" by The Hollies
- "I Know" by Beautiful World
- "Put a Little Love in Your Heart" by Jackie Deshannon
- "Shower The People" by James Taylor
- "Stand by Me" by Ben E. King
- "The Heart of the Matter" by Don Henley
- "The Greatest Love of All" by Whitney Houston
- "You've Got a Friend" by Carole King
- "Rise Up" by The Parachute Club

---

* Indicates inspirational songs to be sung by classes at graduation as well as the Conflict-Resolution Celebration.

4–9. CONFLICT-RESOLUTION DRAMA PRESENTATION

Objective:

Children perform a dramatic presentation using conflict-resolution concepts they have learned.

Materials and Set-Up Needed:

- Eight large pieces of posterboard with a large printed letter on each piece to spell the word "VIOLENCE" (choose colors and sizes of letters so they can be read by everyone in the audience)
- Large room, preferably the gym, if the whole school will be watching
- Drum
- Music (tapes or CD's to sing along with songs from Music Selections in this book)

Additional preparation for the presentation (optional):

- Kids all in black clothes
- Stage and levels with bleachers, if available, created below and on stage
- Spotlights shining (in front of each level of bleachers) on kids
- Masks that glow

Note: If you decide to use the additional items for your presentation, dimming the lights after everyone in the audience is seated creates a dramatic opening to view the glowing masks.

Room Preparation:

The room is decorated with conflict-resolution displays made by the whole school or by the group performing the presentation. Some examples follow.

Heart Globe: Children make a large globe in the shape of a heart. Caption could be "Let's Solve Our Conflicts with Heart!" Peace doves are hung inside the heart with essays on how to think of the other person's feelings in a conflict while looking at the problem from his or her point of view. Or peace globes and doves may be made from papier-mache- mache and the doves then hung to dangle from the globe.

The Peace Ripplers' Ladder: A large peace rippler ladder is displayed on the wall. A child is starting to climb the ladder. A large peace dove is hung above the ladder with the word "peace." Elicit ideas from children about how they can best spread the peace ripple effect to others. Have their own words printed in large type to be displayed beside each rung of the ladder. Some examples of the conflict-solving tips that help create the peace ripple effect are:

- Control our tempers by calming down when angry
- TLC – **T**une in, **L**isten, **C**hoose a solution for both to win

- Put yourself in the other person's shoes
- Respect yourself and respect others
- Be responsible for your own actions
- Use "I" messages; "I feel . . ."

I. Scenario for Beginning of Presentation:

If using spotlights, the lights in the room are dimmed as the spotlights shine on children kneeling with their heads bent down as the *drum rolls.*

Children take turns in pairs standing up and briefly acting out some everyday conflicts given to you by the students in your school. The rest of the children remain kneeling with their heads down as the conflicts are performed. After each pair performs, each child goes back to his or her kneeling positions. Some examples of everyday conflicts that may be used as scenarios are:

- A child makes fun of another child's clothing (or size) followed by the child's slumped head, shoulders, and a sad expression showing the hurt he or she feels.
- A child who has not calmed down and is ready to hit a sibling in a conflict over use of the TV.
- A child with arms crossed looks away from the other child in a conflict over being left out of a group game as the other tries to persuade him or her to use the TLC approach.
- A child bullies another smaller child by mocking the child and taking away his or her sweatshirt. The child being bullied acts passively but is visibly upset. A small group rises up from their kneeling positions to silently watch the child being bullied.

As the everyday conflicts are finished, one child stands up and asks the audience, "What can *I* do to help these kids?"

II. Peace Ripplers Rise Up:

Play "Rise Up" by the Parachute Club, one refrain as they begin to rise. In unison, children on the stage rise up, join hands together and lift their arms high saying, "You can do so much! We're the Peace Ripplers, here to show you how you can spread ripples of peace in our school."

Enter: Four children come in. (If you are using glowing masks, they make a dramatic entrance.) They talk about the way they would like the school to be, with everyone solving their conflicts so that they feel good about the solutions.

Dialogue:

CHILD # 1: "What can we do to make our school *(name)* _____ even better?"

CHILD #2: "We can think of ways to ripple the effect of not giving in or watching any bullying at our school, and trying real hard to solve our conflicts so everyone feels like winners."

CHILD #3: "But sometimes when you just know you're right and you've been treated unfairly, it's too hard to give in to the other person!"

ALL THE KIDS: "Yeah!"

CHILD #4: "Hey, you're all right about that. It *is* hard when you feel you are right to look at the problem from somebody else's shoes. But if you don't try to give in a little you will both end up fighting, maybe hurting each other and getting in trouble instead of resolving your problem. When you think about it, usually nobody is 100% right. Let's spread the ripple effect and try to work things out at school and at home."

ALL THE KIDS: "Hey, we're willing to try."

III. Line Up Against V-I-O-L-E-N-C-E:

Eight children each hold up a letter to spell the word "violence." Each child tells *how he or she feels a word that begins with the letter he or she holds contributes to violence.* For example, a child holding the letter "V" may say a word that contributes to violence that begins with that letter is "vengeance" and explains, "When people want to seek revenge or get even with others, it contributes to violence." Or a child holding the letter "E" may choose the word "envy" as a contributor to violence by saying when people want what others have, they may become violent to obtain the same things. Each child continues until all the letters are held up and the word "violence" is spelled. Together all eight children say, "We *can spread ripples* to stop the violence we see around us."

IV. Conflict-Resolution Skits:

Choose a skit from this book, such as "A Geeky Play" or Wilbert's "sticky situation" skits, or have children in the presentation make up some of their everyday conflicts to role-play.

V. Scenario for Music:

The children on stage lead the audience in a selected song or songs. Refer to the song selections from this book. (A favorite song for this Celebration is "Angels Among Us" by Alabama.) If the children attending the presentation have learned the song ahead of time after being played on the school intercom or in individual classrooms, all may now join in singing with the group on the stage.

Otherwise, the children on the stage perform for the audience. Depending upon the room size and the number of children in the audience, the children may move from the stage to surround the audience while they form a *circle* with their hands held. If the room is large enough, each class could then form circles and each class moves alternately clockwise and counterclockwise while children hold hands and sing together.

VI. Closing of Celebration:

Choose a student to read the poem "We're the Peace Ripplers" from the cover for "My Peace Ripplers Book." The poem could be displayed on an overhead projector for everyone to recite the poem together. This reading will close the Celebration.

PEACE DOVE

This peace dove may be used for a front hall or classroom display. Students write inside the doves what they will do to contribute to a peaceful school. Or poems or essays students write about peace may be attached under the peace doves with each child's name on the doves. All the peace doves are hung in the hall to spell the name of your school or the word "peace."

In addition, you can make peace dove name tags for students for the rotating classroom activities if you have a schoolwide Conflict-Resolution Celebration.

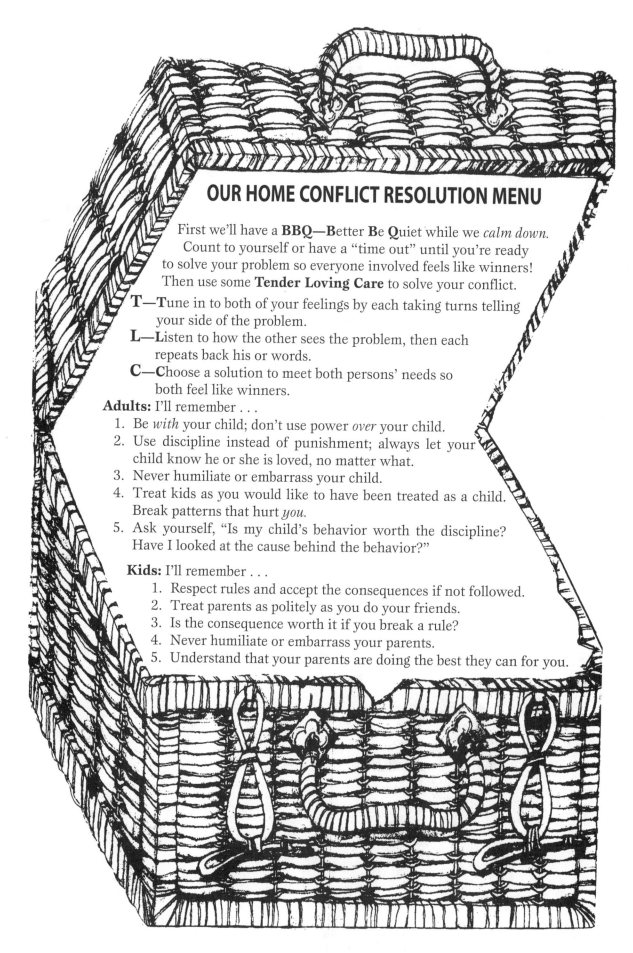

OUR HOME CONFLICT RESOLUTION MENU

First we'll have a **BBQ—B**etter **B**e **Q**uiet while we *calm down*. Count to yourself or have a "time out" until you're ready to solve your problem so everyone involved feels like winners! Then use some **Tender Loving Care** to solve your conflict.

T—Tune in to both of your feelings by each taking turns telling your side of the problem.

L—Listen to how the other sees the problem, then each repeats back his or words.

C—Choose a solution to meet both persons' needs so both feel like winners.

Adults: I'll remember . . .

1. Be *with* your child; don't use power *over* your child.
2. Use discipline instead of punishment; always let your child know he or she is loved, no matter what.
3. Never humiliate or embarrass your child.
4. Treat kids as you would like to have been treated as a child. Break patterns that hurt *you*.
5. Ask yourself, "Is my child's behavior worth the discipline? Have I looked at the cause behind the behavior?"

Kids: I'll remember . . .

1. Respect rules and accept the consequences if not followed.
2. Treat parents as politely as you do your friends.
3. Is the consequence worth it if you break a rule?
4. Never humiliate or embarrass your parents.
5. Understand that your parents are doing the best they can for you.

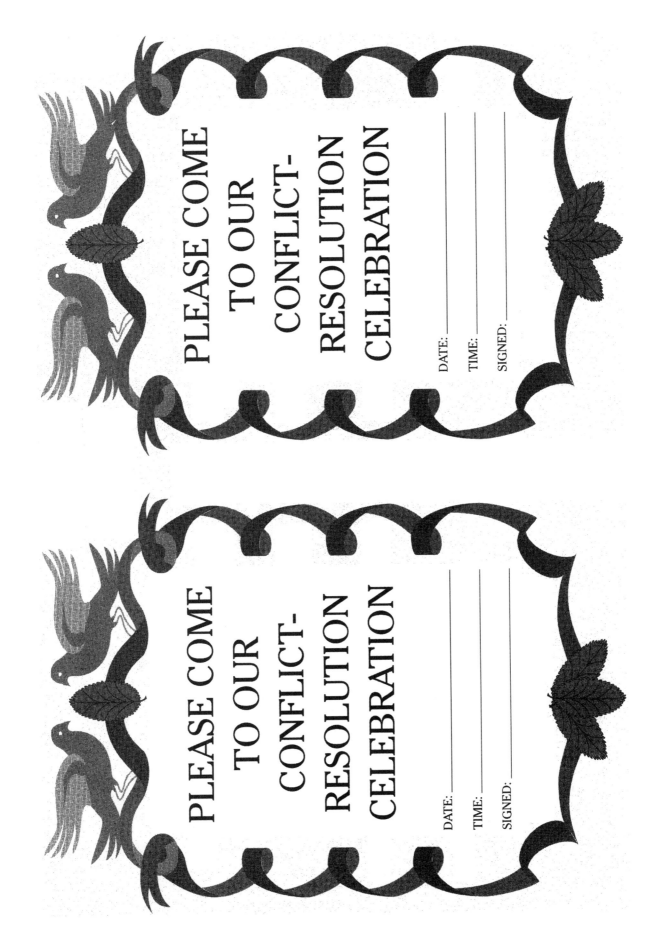

PLEASE COME TO OUR CONFLICT-RESOLUTION CELEBRATION

DATE: _____

TIME: _____

SIGNED: _____

PLEASE COME TO OUR CONFLICT-RESOLUTION CELEBRATION

DATE: _____

TIME: _____

SIGNED: _____

DEAR _____ ,

Here is a heartfelt invitation to you!
At school we are learning how to solve our
conflicts so everyone feels the solution if
fair. We are learning to put ourselves in the
other person's shoes when he or she is hurt and
think how we would feel if it happened to us.

We are having a celebration of all we have learned
to deal with our problems and our anger.
Since we are learning to think about
others' feelings, we are calling it
"Conflict Solving with Heart."

PLEASE COME TO OUR
"CONFLICT SOLVING WITH HEART" CELEBRATION!

DATE: _____ TIME: _____

SIGNED: _____

4–14. GOOD NEWS NETWORK GRAMS
4–15. GOOD NEWS NETWORK CALENDAR
4–16. GOOD NEWS NETWORK MONTHLY THEME IDEAS

Objective:

Children contribute to a feeling of community in the school by having designated days to announce kids' usable "good news."

Materials Needed:

- Faculty interested in having a "Good News Network" and educators willing to edit children's submissions
- Boxes or large envelopes decorated and located in front hall or individual classrooms
- Good News Network grams placed beside boxes or envelopes for student submissions
- Good News Network calendar
- Good News Network Monthly Theme Ideas

Directions:

1. Have a box with "good news" grams in the front hall of your school for students to deposit their ideas for the broadcasts.

2. Alternative to the idea of having a front hall box deposit is to have a box or large hanging envelope in each classroom. Children's submissions are edited by the classroom teacher and then submitted for use in the broadcast to the principal or to the teacher in charge for the month.

3. Decide when and how often your school will have the broadcasts, such as every Monday morning.

4. Perhaps a different teacher could be in charge each month of the submission and choosing of the announcements submitted each week.

5. Do you want to have a different "good news" theme every month? See the "Good News Network Monthly Themes Ideas" for monthly themes and sections from this book you may want to include in the themes. Cut out boxes below for the calendars to indicate the schedule of broadcasts.

Good News Network Broadcast	**Good News Network Broadcast**	**Good News Network Broadcast**	**Good News Network Broadcast**	**Good News Network Broadcast**

GOOD NEWS NETWORK

Date _____

Teacher _____ Grade _____

Good News:_____

_____

_____

_____

_____

GOOD NEWS NETWORK

Date _____

Teacher _____ Grade _____

Good News:_____

_____

_____

_____

_____

GOOD NEWS NETWORK CALENDAR

HERE IS WHAT WE ARE LOOKING FORWARD TO THIS MONTH!

S	M	T	W	T	F	S

GOOD NEWS NETWORK
MONTHLY THEME IDEAS

September:

We Are Family! Month: Kids' give input on setting school and classroom rules, how kids can contribute and what to do about the consequences if not followed. *(Section 2)*

October:

Positive Identity Month: Kids learn how to give compliments to each other for efforts and accomplishments they notice in their peers and themselves. *(Section 2)*

November:

Belonging Month: Future gang affiliation may be discouraged with the children themselves pointing out the value of getting involved in the school, sports, drama or music as opposed to joining gangs to meet their needs for belonging. *(Section 2)*

December:

Multicultural Month: Stories shared about the countries children, their parents, or grandparents came from and sharing of their cultural holiday ideas. *(Section 2)*

January:

Values Month: Make value-instilling a fun, shared event by announcing student submissions about something positive, morals, or lessons they have learned from movies, TV shows, books, or articles they have read that they would like to share with others. *(Section 2)*

GOOD NEWS NETWORK
MONTHLY THEME IDEAS
(continued)

February:

Empathy Month: Caring for and loving others. Sharing stories of putting yourself in somebody else's shoes and making them feel better if they are hurt. *(Section 3)*

March:

Conflict-Resolution Month: Children share their "happy ending" conflict stories with others. *(Sections 3, 4)*

April:

Month of "showers of problems" students give for others to solve creatively! *(Section 3)*

May:

Bully Buster! Month: Positive stories about discouraging bullies. (No names are to be included in these stories. *(Section 4)*

June:

We've Got It All Together! Month: Have a schoolwide celebration with classes rotating to different conflict-resolution activities including classes all coming together to the gym for activities, skits, and songs. *(Section 4)*

CHILL-OUT TIME FOR TWO!

"A caring teacher is more important than any curriculum." Periodic private time with individual students can provide valuable insight into academic performance without necessarily even mentioning a subject or a grade. The teacher's role is that of a nonjudgmental, caring listener. Five or ten minutes spent at the start of recess or lunch may be time well-spent in helping you get to know your students privately. You might want to call it "Time for Two" for primary or junior grades and "Give Me Five!" or "Chill-Out Time" for seniors.

Date	Student	Hobbies/Interests	Sports Favorites	Feelings— Family/Friends	Other

4–18. PLANNING OUR CLASS MEETINGS
4–19. OUR CLASS MEETING MENU

Objective:

Class meetings are events to look forward to and an opportunity for "airing out" problems and grievances in a "no put-down" atmosphere as well as sharing good news.

Materials Needed:

- Regular posting area for children to sign up to be on the menu for the next class meeting (either space on the board or a chart or class meeting menu displayed on the wall.)
- "Our Class Meeting Menu" class sheet

Directions:

1. Be positive when looking forward to these meetings. The children will pick up on your mood! At times, put your own name on the class meeting menu and share one of your own problems and seek problem-solving advice from your students.

2. Decide how often you will hold your class meetings. Do you want to combine them with the day of the week you do *life skills* activities with the children such as self-esteem, creative problem solving, and conflict resolution? Do you want to hold them to brighten up Monday mornings? Let your students know ahead of time so they can sign up to be on the class meeting menu if they wish.

3. Have a class discussion about the ground rules of your class meetings. Have them printed and displayed during meetings so the children know the expectations. Explain that the objective of these meetings is to "air out" problems and to share possible solutions as well as sharing good news with one another. Tell children that class meetings are not tattletale events; in fact, no names are to be mentioned during the meetings or on the sign-up sheet. The problem may be outlined but if it concerns another person, that person or persons' name(s) is not to be mentioned.

   Before students sign their names on the sign-up sheet, they must ask themselves the question, "Can I solve this problem on my own?" If students are able to find a way to solve their problems without class help, they should erase or cross off their names from the class meeting sheet before the meeting begins. Children who sign up for each class meeting with the sole intention of gaining attention for themselves will soon be discouraged if they are asked this question.

4. Discuss with your class your expectations of their empathy for each other during class meetings. These expectations include respect for one another's feelings. They include privacy, respect for others by not talking about the problems outside of the classroom, and no put-downs verbally or with body language. A feeling prevails that "we are all in this together" when a child presents a problem he or she needs help solving.

5. Seating for class meetings should be different from the class's ordinary seating. You may want to decide as a class how the seating will be arranged and where the class

meetings will be held. Circles in the classroom work well for some, whereas a change of rooms is welcome for others.

6. If you want to use the "menu" idea for your class meetings, set the mood by displaying "Our Class Meeting Menu" in your classroom. Divide the meeting into "menu left-overs" to give the opportunity to children who had problems at the last class meeting to give feedback about the way they handled their conflicts and to tell how things are going for them now.

    For the "main course," students who signed up on the sheet take turns talking about their problems or conflicts and others offer some conflict-solving strategies for them. The idea is to have a brainstorming session—and nobody's solution is put down. A recorder could write all the ideas on a chart or board. The best solution is then chosen for the child to use.

    If *you* have a conflict you would like the children to help you solve, sign it under the "main course" next to "Teacher's Chance."

    The end of the meeting can be the "icing on the cake." This should end the meeting *on a sweet* note by having happy news, creative puzzles for the class to solve by the next meeting, or a compliment activity (use an activity from this book, Section 2; such as, "A Positive Identity" or the "Diamonds!" activity from Section 1.")

7. If you choose to end the meeting with a snack, two or three students should sign up to bring a small snack for each meeting, taking into consideration any special dietary concerns any of the students may have. Or perhaps twice yearly the class meeting could end with a snack.

8. If your beginning class meetings are at times discouraging, be patient. Teachers who have succeeded with regularly successful class meetings say they were well worth the effort. They claim that the moments they spent watching the empathy that developed within the children during these class meetings throughout the year provided the reward to them.

OUR CLASS MEETING

See you at our next Class Meeting! It will on _____.

MENU LEFTOVERS:

Kids from **MAIN COURSE** last time can talk about how things have been going since the last class meeting. Are there still any "leftover" problems or did our solutions work?

Before you sign your name for the "Main Course," ask yourself this question:

"Can I solve this problem or work out my conflict with the other person(s) all by myself?"

If you do solve it before the meeting, erase your name. Remember, no other *names* mentioned.

MAIN COURSE:

Problems in your life you'd like some recipes for solutions:

1. _____
2. _____
3. _____
4. _____
5. _____

Teacher's Chance to get a new recipe for: _____

ICING ON THE CAKE:

Do you have happy news, creative puzzles, a "compliment" activity?

1. _____
2. _____
3. _____
4. _____
5. _____

Snack will be brought by: _____

READ MORE ABOUT IT!

Resources to Help You Help Your Students
Learn Now What You Didn't Learn in School

Adler, Mortimer J. *How to Speak How to Listen.* New York: Macmillan Publishing Co., 1983.

Borba, Michele. *Esteem Builders.* Torrance, CA: Jalmar Press, 1995.

Begun, Ruth Weltmann. *Ready-to-Use Social Skills Lessons & Activities for Grades 1–3.* West Nyack, NY: Center for Applied Research in Education, 1995.

_____. *Ready-to-Use Social Skills Lessons & Activities for Grades 4–6.* West Nyack, NY: Center for Applied Research in Education, 1995.

Bloomfield, Harold H. *Making Peace With Your Parents.* New York: Ballantine Books, 1983.

Branden, Nathaniel. *Honoring the Self.* New York: Bantam Books, 1989.

_____. *The Art of Self-Discovery.* New York: Bantam Books, 1993.

Breathnach, Sarah Ban. *Simple Abundance.* New York: Warner Books, 1995.

Canfield, Jack. *The Aladdin Factor.* New York: The Berkley Publishing Group, 1995.

Canfield, Jack and Mark Hansen. *Chicken Soup for the Soul: A Reader's Library.* Deerfield Beach, FL: Health Communications, Inc., 1993.

Canter, Lee and Marlene Canter. *Assertive Discipline.* Santa Monica, CA: Lee Canter & Associates, 1976.

Chase, Larry. *The Other Side of the Report Card: How-to-Do-It Program for Affective Education.* Santa Monica, CA: Goodyear Publishing Co., 1994.

Childre Doc Lew. *Freeze Frame.* Boulder Creek, CA: Planetary Publications, 1994.

Clinton, Hillary Rodham. *It Takes a Village.* New York: Simon & Schuster, 1996.

Coloroso, Barbara. *Kids Are Worth It!* Toronto: Somerville House Publishing, 1994.

De Bono, Edward. *Serious Creativity.* Toronto: HarperCollins, 1992.

Dennison, Susan. *Creating Positive Support Group Curriculums for At-Risk Children.* Torrance, CA: Jalmar Press, 1997.

Dreikurs, Rudolf and Pearl Cassel. *Discipline Without Tears.* New York: Hawthorn Books, 1972.

_____. *Children: The Challenge.* New York: Dutton, 1987.

Drew, Naomi. *Learning the Skills of Peacemaking.* Torrance, CA: Jalmar Press, 1996.

Dyer, Wayne. *What Do You Really Want for Your Children?* New York: Avon Books, 1985.

Elkind, David. *The Hurried Child.* Reading, MA: Addison-Wesley, 1992.

_____. *Ties That Stress: The New Family Imbalance.* Cambridge, MA: Harvard University Press, 1994.

Faber, Adele and Elaine Mazlish. *How to Talk So Kids Will Listen & Listen So Kids Will Talk.* New York: Avon Books, 1980.

Freeman, Arthur and Rose DeWolf. *Woulda, Coulda, Shoulda.* New York: HarperPerennial, 1989.

Gibbs, Jeanne. *Tribes. A Process for Social Development and Cooperative Learning.* Santa Rosa, CA: Prima Publishing & Communications, 1987.

Glasser, William. *The Quality School.* New York: HarperCollins, 1992.

_____. *Control Theory in the Classroom.* New York: Harper & Row, 1986.

Glenn, H. Stephen and Robert Reasoner. *Developing Capable Young People.* Sacramento, CA: Prima Publishing, 1998.

Goulston, Mark and Philip Goldberg. *Get Out of Your Own Way.* New York: Perigree, 1996.

Heldmann, Mary Lynne. *When Words Hurt.* New York: Ballantine Books, 1988.

Helmstetter, Shad. *The Self-Talk Solution.* New York: Pocket Books, 1987.

Hendrix, Harville. *Giving the Love That Heals.* New York: Pocket Books, 1997.

Holt, John. *How Children Fail.* New York: Dell Publishing, 1982.

Johnson, David W. and Roger T. Johnson. *Creative Conflict.* Minneapolis: Cooperative Learning Center ,1987.

Kreidler, William J. *Creative Conflict Resolution.* Glenview, IL: Goodyear Books, 1984.

Lerner, Harriet. *The Dance of Anger.* New York: Perennial Library, 1986.

Loomans, Diane. *Full Esteem Ahead.* Tiburoun, CA: H.J. Kramer, 1994.

Nagel, Greta. *The Tao of Teaching.* New York: Donald I. Fine, Inc., 1994.

Nelson, Jane. *Positive Discipline.* New York: Ballantine Books, 1987.

Nelson, Jane, Lynn Lott and H. Stephen Glenn. *Positive Discipline in the Classroom.* Rocklin, CA: Prima Publishing, 1993.

Pipher, Mary. *Reviving Ophelia.* New York: Ballantine Books, 1994.

Reasoner, Robert. *Building Self-Esteem: A Comprehensive Program.* Palo Alto, CA: Consulting Psychologists Press, 1982.

Rosenburg, Marshall. *Non-Violent Communicaiton: A Language of Compassion.* Torrance, CA: Jalmar Press, 1997.

Siegel, Bernie S. *Peace, Love & Healing.* New York: HarperCollins, 1992.

Simon, Sidney B. *Getting Unstuck.* New York: Warner Books, Inc., 1988.

Simon, Sidney B. and Sally Olds. *Helping Your Child Learn Right From Wrong.* New York: McGraw-Hill, 1976.

Sloane, Paul. *Lateral Thinking Puzzles.* New York: Sterling Publishing Co., 1992.

Sloane, Paul and Des McHale. *Challenging Lateral Thinking Puzzles.* New York: Sterling Publishing Co., 1993.

Teolis, Beth. *Ready-to-Use Self-Esteem & Conflict-Solving Activities for Grades 4–8.* West Nyack, NY: Center for Applied Research in Education, 1996.

Waas, Lane Longino. *Imagine That! Getting Smarter Through Imagery Practice.* Torrance, CA: Jalmar Press, 1995.

Waitley, Denis. *Being the Best.* New York: Pocket Books, 1987.

Williams, Redford and Virginia Williams. *Anger Kills.* New York: HarperCollins, 1993.

NOTES

NOTES

NOTES

NOTES

NOTES

NOTES

NOTES

NOTES

NOTES